# FIRING BACK

# FIRING BACK

## Power Strategies for Cutting the Best Deal When You're About to Lose Your Job

Jodie-Beth Galos
Sandy McIntosh, Ph.D.

John Wiley & Sons, Inc.

New York • Chichester • Weinheim • Brisbane • Singapore • Toronto

*Library of Congress Cataloging-in-Publication Data*

Galos, Jodie-Beth.
    Firing back : power strategies for cutting the best deal when
you're about to lose your job / Jodie-Beth Galos, Sandy McIntosh.
        p.   cm.
    Includes index.
    ISBN 0-471-18031-9 (pbk. alk. paper)
    1.   Severance pay—United States.   I. McIntosh, Sandy.   II. Title.
HD4928.D5G35   1997
658.3'222   dc20                                            96-46167

Printed in the United States of America

10  9  8  7  6  5  4  3  2  1

# AUTHORS' NOTE

The real-life stories in this book, selected to illustrate common issues rather than private lives, are told in the voices of real people, with some alterations made for literary and privacy purposes. Every effort has been made, to the best of the authors' ability, to keep privacy intact. The effort to protect individuals' privacy may inadvertently result in a description of a real person unknown to the authors. Any such resemblance is purely coincidental.

# CONTENTS

## PART THREE

### THE NEGOTIATIONS

# ACKNOWLEDGMENTS

The authors wish to thank the following friends, colleagues, and (formerly) complete strangers who took the time to read, listen to us complain about whatever was on our minds, and in spite of that, offer us their expert advice: Dick Block, Dodge Dutcher, Aaron Edelman, Ellen Fernandez, Joel Finger, Shelley Freeman, Dan Greenberg (our agent), Chris Jackson (our editor), Pam Pearson, Joe Plumeri, Jeff Rosenberg, Karen Ruef, Bob Schulman, Gary Thompson, and Bob Vavrina—and all the people who told us their stories under a guarantee of anonymity.

To those near and dear to us—Michael, Shirley, George, Maria, and Barbara—we owe another kind of debt entirely, mainly for staying out of our way so we could finish the book.

*"I'll lay it out for you. We're cutting back, and
we no longer need a dog."*

Drawing by Weber; © 1979 The New Yorker Magazine, Inc.

# INTRODUCTION

The only thing worse than imagining this scene is having to act it out for real: One Friday afternoon, at the end of the day, you're called into your boss's office. Seated behind the desk, wearing a somber expression, is your employer, or perhaps a stranger from human resources.

She explains the situation to you: "*. . . and so, I regret to inform you that your job is being eliminated. You will be given a separation package and you must clear out your office immediately.*"

How do you react? Here's one way:

JODIE-BETH (*thinking furiously*): "This is the most embarrassing thing that's ever happened in my life. How will I tell my family? They'll think I'm a failure. I know! As I usually do, I'll get dressed in the morning for work and go sit in the park for eight hours. Maybe they'll never figure it out. Separation pay? *I'll* pay the company to keep my disgrace a secret."

Here's another way:

SANDY (*leaping to his feet and shouting*): "You can't terminate me! Severance? Take your crummy package and shove it! I'll sue! I'll go to the press! You won't get away with this! I've worked too hard and long. Where's my gun? I'm barricading myself in my office. Come and get me, you wimp!"

Perhaps you're more levelheaded than either of us. You might choose, instead, to accept your fate quietly, even graciously. After all, what else can you do? Employers set the rules and you must obey them. You're terminated; you have no options.

1

Or so it seems. *It's true you've lost your job; it's false you have no options.*

The reality of the American workplace in the 1990s is that employees, individually or in crowds, have been, are being, and will be terminated as companies scramble to shore up shaky bottom lines. To an excited media—and to you, too, if you're finding yourself looking down the wrong end of the termination gun barrel—this might represent a profound change in the traditional covenant between employer and employee. Workers who in the past could look forward to serving one or two employers during their adult careers must now regard their present jobs as merely transitional. On the other hand, some observers find the present employment climate to be business as usual; nothing new here. Workers have always been subject to the whims of their employers—there's just less sugarcoating on that unpalatable truth these days.

In the recent corporate downsizing debates, journalists, politicians, and famous CEOs have offered analysis and sympathy to departing workers. They've paid little attention, however, to a *crucial* point in the employment relationship—the actual moment of termination.

Contrary to the nearly universal notion that termination is the stigmatizing hour of shame, leaving employees with their backs against the wall and no room to negotiate, the termination meeting and the subsequent severance negotiations offer employees unique opportunities to take back control of their futures—provided they know how.

Termination isn't the result of supernatural forces beyond your control. The same company that hired you, and with whom you've been able to deal with such things as office space, salary, and vacations, is also the company that wants you gone. You were able to work with them previously because you each had something to gain and something to lose. Now, at the end of your business relationship, the situation is the same: They want you out, but it's up to you to make it worth your while to go.

*Firing Back* brings expertise to this issue. This book is aimed at employees who need new skills in order to effectively negotiate their hirings and firings within complex legal and financial constraints.

This is a book about how to stop acting like a victim and start taking control—control of your present work situation; control of your termination (if that's inevitable); control of the subsequent separation negotiations; control of your finances, savings, and investments;

and, finally, control of your future. To be told you can control all this right now may seem an improbability—especially if, at the moment, you're without a clue to your immediate fate. But get comfortable. We're going to show you how to regain control, step-by-step.

## HOW TO USE THIS BOOK

We've organized *Firing Back* to be used in a crisis. In each chapter we've bulleted topics and flagged urgent information with a ☞. You'll find the information you need right now by going directly to it without having to wade through pages of theoretical ruminations.

**If you suspect your job is in jeopardy,** *or if you know it is,* **turn to Part One.** There you'll find key danger signs that forecast a termination, a list of the things you'll need to do to prepare for it, and a move-by-move game plan to help you set up the termination meeting as a springboard for your next moves—CHAPTER THREE IS MUST READING!

**If you've already been terminated but haven't met with your employer to work out your separation package, concentrate on Parts Two and Three.** A separation agreement does not have to be a one-sided affair, with terms dictated by your boss. In fact, we'll show you that your bargaining position is surprisingly strong. We'll walk you through the steps you'll need to take in order to effectively research and analyze your negotiating position. We'll help you calculate your financial needs and examine the monetary and nonmonetary items that will improve your separation package. We'll bring you up to speed on employment law, and help you decide whether you'll benefit from legal counsel. We'll also remove the mystery from an often-confusing employer requirement: the termination settlement and release. We recommend you read through these parts entirely before you begin your separation negotiations to get an overview of the separation negotiation process.

Most important, these chapters will teach you how to be an effective negotiator. You may not think you have that capability now, but we'll take it apart for you and put it back together, and by the time you finish reading, you won't feel like a victim in the negotiating process.

**If you've already worked out a separation agreement—for**

**good or for ill—and you're ready to get on with your personal
and professional life, turn to Part Four.** Before you do anything
else, you should get a handle on some financial essentials. These
include replacing insurance, maximizing your employer-sponsored
benefits, and investing your separation money. We'll then point you
in the right direction for your next job. We'll guide you through a
review of the hidden traps that may have snared you in your last job,
so that you'll recognize them in your next. We'll also suggest a new
mental attitude to consider adopting to situate you both psychologi-
cally and financially in a position that promises success: the attitude
of the personally responsible entrepreneur.

The strategies we offer in this book are incisive, powerful, and
effective. They're based on several premises that you should think
about: First, that anyone can be terminated for reasons both fair and
unfair, and that termination itself presents the opportunity to improve
your fortunes, not lose them; second, that employees, while not standing on exactly equal footing with their employer in negotiations, can
bring significant leverage to bear; and, third, that negotiations that
are professional, even cordial in tone, while extremely tough-minded
around the issues are the most effective. Nothing of what we offer in
this book is predicated on the desire for revenge, unless you consider,
as we do, that success is the best possible revenge.

# PART ONE

# TERMINATION

# 1

# TROUBLE BREWING

Long before an actual termination, you get the feeling that odd things are happening. Rumors fly back and forth across the employee grapevine. There's a definite suspicion that *something* is going on, something upsetting. And perhaps there's some suspicion, too, about who's going to be upset. In order to determine what that something is and if you are the someone it will affect, examine yourself and your world for the telltale signs of change. Is the threat real, or is it only your vague paranoia setting off alarms?

## READING THE SIGNS OF CHANGE IN YOUR JOB SECURITY

To begin, check yourself. If you've been flipping through this book and you're reading with more than casual interest, it's probably accurate to assume you sense something in the works threatening your security. You may have chosen to ignore it or at least diminish its significance, but *something* is going on. Look for one or more of these clear signs that will tell you that your job security is threatened:

- Changes in the behavior of your co-workers, subordinates, and boss
- Changes in job performance feedback
- Changes in your assignments and responsibilities
- Changes in your perks
- Changes in company management
- Changes in the company's financial position

These signs can appear individually or all at once. Try to identify them as objectively and unemotionally as possible.

## Changes in the Behavior of Your Co-workers, Subordinates, and Boss

Study the behavior of your co-workers. In an ideal world governed by a benevolent and protective team spirit, you might expect someone to warn you if he or she knew your number was up. Abandon this belief. Despite corporate myths fostered by expensive, time-devouring employee "teamwork" programs, your co-workers do not constitute an extended family. Real families do not downsize their members: *"Sorry, son. Your mother and I have been talking, and we think that there are too many layers between us and the dog. Keep in touch; if something opens up, we'll do lunch."* Don't be surprised or disappointed when your co-workers put their self-interest first and politely (or less than politely) ignore you and your plight. Your co-workers have concluded that you have a dread disease called *bad luck* or *failure*, and they're afraid whatever you've got is catching.

Here are the changes to look for:

- You aren't invited to relevant meetings and aren't sent pertinent memos, or your memos are given limited distribution.
- Decisions are made without your input but with the input of your peers or subordinates.
- People who formerly asked your permission or advice are not asking you now.
- Information from your boss or your peers is given to your subordinates before it's given to you.

The most important co-worker to observe for changes in attitude toward you is your boss. If your boss is feeling either remorse or relief, he or she will behave differently than in the past. An unpleasant human being who, startlingly, becomes pleasant is just as dangerous as one who does the reverse. In most cases, however, the behavior to look for in your boss is his avoidance of you. Guilt and fear are often a boss's emotions in anticipating a termination.

Strange as this may sound, some of the best indicators of a change in status can come from secretaries. That's because they're often the people who either type up the documents critical to employees' futures, or they overhear good information. Check it out—are you given a cooler greeting from your boss's secretary? Worse yet, do you detect a new note of sympathy in his or her voice?

☞ Be cautious in your search for information about your job security. You are after information, so you should be listening; someone else should be talking.

Don't confide your fears to co-workers, no matter how close you feel to them or how trustworthy they've been in the past. Your situation has changed, and it will do you no good to validate suspicions that you are on a hit list. Instead, give someone the chance to deliver the bad news to you. Whatever else this says about human nature, it might make someone's day.

## Changes in Job Performance Feedback

If you've received an oral or written warning, or a poor performance appraisal, this may be a prelude to termination. It's a mistake to ignore these, because no supervisor ever enjoys giving them. If your supervisor has made an honest effort to alert you to your doom, you should regard your situation as serious. Even if the warning seems mild to you, don't disregard it. Most warnings are kinder than the harsher reality. They may be worded ambiguously because the writer or speaker is uncomfortable, inexperienced, or both at giving bad news.

Sometimes, a change in performance feedback is far from an honest attempt to give you notice. It's not beyond a sneaky supervisor to file a poor performance appraisal as a setup for termination. Keep in mind, however, that performance appraisals and other forms of documentation will serve as effective "paper trails" for the company only if they report the truth, the whole truth. If, in fact, the event described didn't happen or happened differently from the way it was documented, it will hurt the company's position. It means someone has lied to set you up because he or she couldn't fault you any other way. Whenever you're given a document to sign that you don't agree with, either don't sign it or sign it under protest and place a rebuttal in your file. Remember that your salary history

## Notes from the Firing Line

*A record of commendations for the good work you've done over the years can turn the tables on a dishonest employer:*

I had worked for my company for more than twenty years when I was suddenly fired. Ironically, on the way back to my office after being told that it was in my best interests to "step down" from my job, the head of our Public Affairs office met me in the hallway. "Steve," he said, extending his hand. "My best congratulations!" I must have looked shell-shocked, so he explained what he meant. "Didn't you get my note?" "What note?" I asked. "The note I sent letting you know you'd been given your Service Recognition Award—a nice little Tiffany clock," he added.

I went home to think about it all. What did my boss mean, it was in my "best interests" to leave the company? I didn't think it was in my best interests. My family didn't think it was in my best interests, and my attorney certainly didn't think it was in my best interests. So, I filed a lawsuit and got busy going through my files.

I had saved twenty years of commendation letters from the chairman on down. I had kept all the little invitations to parties, golf weekends, and other celebrations that I was invited to as thanks for my job performance over the years. I also had pictures of me wearing black tie, having my hand shaken as I was given this, that, or some other plaque for meritorious service. The best piece of evidence in my collection was a personal note from the guy who fired me, complimenting me on another year of stellar performance. (All the people who joked over the years that I kept every scrap of paper I'd ever received aren't chuckling now.)

In court the company argued that a monkey given my sales territory could have done as well or better. My attorney pointed out that the company should have placed a monkey in the job a lot sooner, as opposed to leaving me there for twenty years. It would have saved them all the money for awards and citations they'd given me, even in the year I was fired. I, of course, won.

—Steve, sales, age 61

speaks volumes about your job performance, and evidence of flattering raises can be used to refute the harsh words of a written warning. It's obviously suspicious when a warning is suddenly given to an employee who has had years of satisfactory performance reviews and good salary increases. If this happens to you, you'll be able to point out this inherently contradictory and questionable documentation, supporting your position that the "setup" was engineered by your supervisor.

☞ If you're slated to be part of a no-fault termination, such as a layoff, you may not be given advance feedback about poor job performance. Some companies consider information about job performance when selecting employees for a layoff; other companies use tenure or position to make a sufficiently fair and business-focused decision.

## Changes in Assignments and Responsibilities

Many people, sensing the winds of change, are quick to deny to themselves that they may be blown away. People in denial protest that a change in responsibility or assignment is either meaningless or actually for the good. They're only right when the change increases their responsibilities or provides them with exciting new assignments. Loss of responsibility is never good, no matter how flatteringly the change is presented. If your contribution is truly valued, the best way to liberate your time would be to have the task assigned to someone who reports to you. That enhances you, enabling you to provide guidance and input.

☞ Be wary when you are told that the change will free you for more productive tasks. People who are being groomed for bigger roles are usually given more responsibility, not less.

## Changes in Perks

There's a message being delivered when tokens of esteem are taken from you and given to others: Others are in favor and you're not.

## Notes from the Firing Line

*When you're given less to do instead of more, your prospects for success with your present company are dim:*

I knew I was in trouble when my mentor was let go following a management change. Suddenly, I was reporting to Mr. Administrivia. The first thing he asked me to do was write up a job description of what I do. When we sat down to review my job description, his only comment was, "Wow, Sarah, I didn't know you did all this stuff." Who did he think did it all? Elvis?

Two days later, he came into my office to tell me that we needed to talk. He had that sad, burden-of-authority look that reminded me of Wally Cleaver's father. He told me that after much deliberation, he felt my job scope was too broad. "Sarah," he concluded, "I want you to play in a smaller sandbox. Let's see how that suits you."

I suggested that he wouldn't have made that kind of debasing comment to a man. He panicked, and called in human resources. The next thing I knew, we're talking about my long-term career objectives in an ominous sort of way. I decided that my long-term career would be better served by taking a generous separation package now from these people and finding myself a new employer—someone who would not be overly threatened if I were to play in the big sandbox.

—Sarah, communications executive, age 38

Many medium-to-large companies are so bureaucratic that perks—office size and position, parking access, paid club memberships, and so on—are institutionalized to the point where they don't change despite the changing status of employees or the company itself. You could be lucky and work at a place where the largesse isn't carefully regulated and *real* perks are provided to those who are well regarded.

Being close to the locus of power is always better than being out of the loop. Sitting in an office close to your boss is good. Being sent to parking lot Siberia is not good, and it seldom happens accidentally.

☞ If you question your loss of perks and privileges, and you're told that the new rule is "no exceptions," scrutinize your environment. Exceptions are how the favored few receive confirmation that they are the favored few.

## Changes in Management

Managers entering a new job are often clueless as to what they should do first. Since new managers seldom are hired to continue the work of their predecessors, they feel pressured to take action to justify their existence. Rolling a few heads, particularly those associated with the old regime, often seems to be a logical first move.

If your new boss is asking you for your views on the company's past, it's a good sign. If your new boss is asking you for your views on the future, it's a better sign. If your new boss is taking your subordinates to breakfast, it's a bad sign.

## Changes in the Company's Position

As you review the signs of change, you may conclude that you, personally, are in good shape. In that case, it may be your company that's in jeopardy. If your company is in a downturn, it could mean problems for you. Some of the more obvious signs include revenue reductions and budget cuts, which often translate as job eliminations. Other problems include changes in technology or new market advances that render your company's products and your specialty obsolete. Bad news on a corporate level can affect your job security on a personal level. Companies that survive major strikes or work stoppages are often forced to take drastic steps to return to normalcy. Bad news about a product's performance in the market may result in work curtailment, and downsizings can accompany a corporate merger or acquisition. For some people, a corporate restructuring presents unfettered opportunity; for many more, it's the nightmare version of the children's game of musical chairs, with the spoiled brat of your childhood memory unseating you.

Be aware of these potentially dangerous signs of corporate change:

* Unannounced meetings on strange or seemingly unimportant topics

- Unexplained absences of the company's senior executives
- Discussions about budget changes and expense cutting beyond what would occur normally
- Projects that were important before but are mysteriously put on indefinite hold
- Hiring freezes
- Product offerings that are failing or withdrawn
- Stock market fluctuations or other market actions
- Industry news and rumors of takeovers or mergers

While layoffs resulting from an acquisition may affect you, they are seldom intended as personal criticism of your job performance. You may be an innocent bystander caught up in something bigger than you. On the other hand, it's not impossible that someone has been waiting for an opportunity to get rid of you. *To management, a layoff often seems the perfect place to stash some bodies.* Unlike a firing, a layoff doesn't require the demonstration of faulty job performance, which an employee might refute by an exemplary work history. In a layoff, because there appears to be no individual fault—it's a catastrophe affecting a large group of people—employees are more likely to accept minimal separation packages, sign releases that relinquish the right to sue, and leave quietly, believing there was nothing they could do.

## What Happens If You Ignore the Signs That Something Is Wrong?

There's a great temptation in an unstable work situation for you to ignore the signals, hoping that the problems will miraculously disappear. They won't. Worse yet, ignoring the signals contributes to the possibility that you won't have time to cut the best deal for yourself. Time isn't necessarily on your side. Your assertive response can preserve options, or at least buy you additional time. If nothing else, ignoring the problem leaves you unprepared—and preparation is vital to your negotiating strategy. One of the most important things you can control is your response to what's going on around you. Ignoring the telltale signs that you are about to be terminated cuts into the hours you have to mount your cause. Follow the principles and procedures we'll outline for you, don't give up, and learn how to come to your own rescue.

## Notes from the Firing Line

*If you suspect your company is using the excuse of a mass layoff to sweep you under the carpet, don't capitulate easily:*

I was part of a company that was acquired by another. My boss was laid off and I reported to someone from the new company. One day at lunch, my new boss asked me whether I had had a sexual relationship with my prior boss. I was deeply offended and told him so, intimating that I might even speak with an attorney. A month later, a big downsizing was announced, and my department was hit hard. I wasn't surprised when I was told that my job was being eliminated, because so many other people were losing their jobs. But I also suspected that my new boss was covering up for his unlawful remark. When they gave me my release to get my severance pay, I showed it to my sister-in-law, who's an attorney. She told me I was holding the winning lotto ticket. I had been sexually harassed and treated in a discriminatory manner. I only began to believe it when she represented me and was able to more than triple my severance pay.

—Janet, nurse, age 37

# 2

# PULLING YOURSELF TOGETHER

You've recognized the signs of danger, and you've concluded that your worst fears are real: Your job is in jeopardy. Sooner or later, you assume, the ax will fall. You'll be told your services are no longer needed. Must you meekly accept your firing and any separation package offered by your employer? NO!

☞ Remember that *employment is a two-way street bounded by negotiation.* This may seem to be only wishful thinking at the moment, but as much as your employer has the power to affect your position, you have the power to affect your employer's.

You negotiated to get your job (no matter how actively—or passively), and in one way or another you'll negotiate to give it up. Forfeiting your share of negotiating power would be a needless and regrettable error. Worse, perhaps, would be the blow to your self-esteem. Giving up without a fight in such a crucial area of your life would produce negative results in your personal, family, and community existence. On the other hand, standing up for yourself now will empower you.

## KNOW YOUR RELATIONSHIP WITH YOUR COMPANY

How can you meet your employer on equal ground, as someone whose positions must be accorded sincerity and respect, now

16

and throughout the balance of the relationship? *The key is research.* If possible, before the termination meeting, but certainly before any separation talks, you'll need to do some careful fact-gathering. Your objective is to develop a clear picture of your relationship with the company. Having this will allow you to act with confidence.

Your research will ultimately show you four things:

1. What the company wants from you
2. What the company is prepared to offer you in compensation
3. What you want from the company
4. What you're prepared to offer the company in order to get what you want

## PREPARING FOR
## THE TERMINATION

In this chapter we'll direct you to the information you'll need to face your boss and to anticipate the company's unadorned separation pay offer.

To get started, you should progressively tackle these crucial tasks:

- Resolve to be calm, professional, and businesslike.
- Review your personnel file.
- Review the company's employee handbook and any summary plan descriptions.
- Make friends with someone in your human resources department.
- Make friends with others who know the company's past practices.
- Investigate and research openly.
- Organize your finances so you're aiming for the right exit package.
- Start your documentation of the events and any violations.
- Consider reviewing your situation with a labor lawyer.
- Start your job search.
- Control the timing.

## Resolve to Be Calm, Professional, and Businesslike

A common fault of human beings is that we spend much of our lives offended and angry about real or imagined insults. Our bosses are often the biggest offenders, but now isn't the time to obsess about your boss's demise. At this point, any grave you dig with a wildly emotional shovel will likely be your own. *Master your anxiety.* Whether you choose to confide in your friends and family, attorney, accountant, a professional counselor, or your dog, examine your feelings, get your emotions in check. An over- or undersized ego ruled by anger or fear will be a liability. Check it at the door.

## Review Your Personnel File

In many states, laws give employees the right to check their personnel files at reasonable intervals. Some employers explicitly create that right for employees and note it in their employee handbook. At the time of writing, the following states require employees be given access to their personnel files:

| | | |
|---|---|---|
| Arkansas | Maine | Oregon |
| California | Massachusetts | Pennsylvania |
| Connecticut | Michigan | Rhode Island |
| Delaware | Minnesota | Washington |
| Illinois | Nevada | Wisconsin |
| Kentucky | New Hampshire | |

The rationale for reviewing the contents of your personnel file is NOT to find The Smoking Gun Memo—you know, the one that says *"We need to fire John Doe because he's an old guy who earns too much money and replace him with a young minority woman so that we can meet our affirmative action hiring goals while cutting our payroll costs."* Sorry; only in the movies; you'll never discover that memo in real life.

Your mission in the review of your personnel file is to be sure that it contains no surprises and to judge whether the information is accurate or defamatory, that is, inaccurate and harmful. If asked about your sudden desire to review your file, say that you want to review your employment history because you're applying for a mortgage, checking out your beneficiaries, updating your will.

☞ Be sure to make and keep copies of any documentation the company may use to support your termination if it's based on substandard job performance. Make an inventory of the contents of your file, and either photocopy any warnings or performance appraisals, or at least take a good set of notes about comments critical of your work, as well as those complimentary to it. The more recent the data, the more relevant it is, so note dates.

Be especially attentive to what's *not* in your personnel file. If you find that the company has retrospectively loaded your file with critical records (bad performance reviews, letters of complaint from clients or co-workers, warning notices), you'll want to document the point in time—in all probability, slightly before your departure—when your file suddenly acquired key documents that support your dismissal. Your objective is to show that the company has wholly manufactured evidence against you, or at least has had to grasp for straws. Either of these hasty actions, when proved, will damage the company's credibility.

There shouldn't be anything in your personnel file that you haven't personally reviewed—even if, upon review, you don't agree with the contents. If you find something that you weren't aware of previously—for example, a letter of complaint from a customer or co-worker—note it carefully. If you've placed a letter of rebuttal to performance warnings or appraisals that you thought were inaccurate or unfair, check that the rebuttal is still in the file. If you arranged for a negative appraisal to be removed from a file after you successfully completed a probationary period, make sure it's been removed. If it hasn't been, make a note about its continuing presence in contravention of the agreement between you and the company.

☞ Request in writing that the human resources department and your supervisor correct any inaccurate information you find in your file. Don't forget to check mundane things such as the accuracy of your length of service, your address, number of dependents, and your benefit plan beneficiaries. It should go without saying that any information that you've provided be truthful.

## Review the Company's Employee Handbook
## and Summary Plan Descriptions

The employee handbook is often an overrated document. The real benefits provided by an employer are seldom set forth for everyone to read. Because courts have held that employee handbooks may create an employment contract, companies frequently leave a lot of white space on the pages. But your employee handbook will give you an idea of the minimum benefits available and what the company will likely offer as a starting point in your separation discussions. Summary plan descriptions (SPDs)—written descriptions of benefit programs that give the specifics of who qualifies for the program, what they get, when they get it, and so forth— are legally mandated under the Employee Retirement Income Security Act of 1974 (ERISA) and most large companies have one on their severance pay plan. If you don't have a copy of the severance SPD or any of the other benefit programs in which you have participated, request a copy in writing. If you have copies of the SPDs, check with the human resources department to ensure that the copies are the most current ones. By law, your employer must provide you with an SPD upon your written request; failure to do so will subject your employer to daily fines. When you review these plans, look for schedules of the amounts to be paid upon termination and exceptions to those schedules. (For example, an employee fired for misconduct, such as theft, may be precluded from receiving the benefits provided to employees terminated for lesser offenses.)

Try to obtain the handbook and SPDs in effect at the time you were hired, along with others that might have been issued during your tenure with the company. While the law on this issue is not generally favorable to employees, it may help to show that policies have changed materially for the worse over the years, or that onerous provisions were inserted into policies during your employment, and that no separate consideration was extended to you to agree to these new policies. You may want to argue that the company, in effect, coerced you into accepting these changes.

Also try to obtain a copy of the supervisory manual issued by the human resources department. Sometimes it contradicts what's said in the employee handbook or elaborates on policies in useful ways. Since you should never take a supervisory manual from your employer following termination—it's proprietary material—you should become thoroughly familiar with it now.

## Make Friends with Someone in the Human Resources Department

This is the time to cultivate a friendship with someone in the human resources department. Arranging to have a chat over a cup of coffee would be a move in the right direction. Ask for information and advice—don't engage in policy debates. Human resources departments are seldom powerful enough to set policy; they only administer it. If you don't like the severance policy in the employee handbook, don't take it out on your new friend.

Instead, learn whether anyone was previously able to present compelling circumstances that warranted an exception to the usual policy. Make notes on the human resources person's advice, but do so only after the meeting so that you don't make your new friend feel uneasy.

## Make Friends with Others Who Know the Company's Past Practices

The employee handbook and severance summary plan description represent the company's low-ball position, the minimum guarantees. You now want to learn the best-case scenario, not the worst. People who have left the company will be important contacts, as will be those co-workers who have seen it all and have a historical perspective. Learn as much as you can about exceptions to company policy. *If the written policy represents only minimum assurances, suggest that the real policy is embodied in the unwritten practices.*

## Investigate and Research Openly

At this point you might be concerned that all this questioning will draw attention to you and prompt an immediate and premature termination. Don't be. If someone asks about your sudden interest in your personnel file and benefits, respond as we suggested above or

---

### Notes from the Firing Line

*You'll learn more about the real policy of your company through the experiences of friends:*

When I left my company, it was based upon "mutual agreement." I'm told by a lot of people that's as good as admitting that you've been fired, but in my case it really was a mutual agreement. I thought the job was dead end, and it didn't pay anything close to top dollar. I also felt pretty confident that I had a good reputation in my field and I'd have only a couple of weeks at the most when I'd be unemployed. I approached my boss and we agreed that she'd get me severance even though I had technically resigned. After I left, I started to get phone calls from all kinds of people. At first I was touched, because I thought they were trying to keep the lines of communication open. Then I realized that they were just trying to cut their own deals and wanted to know how I did with mine. I don't tell strangers, but I can't ignore my friends, so I can't say precisely that I've kept it a big secret.

—Bob, graphic artist, age 31

---

say simply that you want to make sure information about you is accurate and current.

If you're mistaken in your worries about sudden unemployment, and your boss wonders about your curiosity, it's likely he or she will confirm that your fears are groundless.

And if your fears have some basis in fact, asking questions won't determine your fate—it's already been decided. All you're signaling is that you're aware of what's going on and preparing to take action. This may even generate a little caution on their part about dealing with you too high-handedly.

### Organize Your Finances So You're Aiming for the Right Exit Package

How should you approach the coming negotiations with your employer? You could decide that your best bet is merely to improve the initial separation offer. You might reason that any increase in the package is a victory—and you'd be right. But this is a lazy, short-sighted goal. You have no way of knowing whether you are leaving money on the table.

Conversely, you could enter negotiations with the objective of making your employer pay through the nose for the terrible harm done you. While this approach at least has focus, it's based on emotion and not on reality. Argued from this standpoint, you would close off the possibility of getting a fair settlement in your headlong rush for retribution.

☞ Your realistic and obtainable objective is to forge a separation package that acts as a secure bridge between your living expenses and your current savings.

Putting it plainly, you must calculate how long you can go without a paycheck before you have to resort to eating the cat's food. Determine which elements of the enhanced separation package are expendable and usable as bargaining chips and which elements are cast in stone and nonnegotiable.

---

### Notes from the Firing Line

*In many cases your employer will accommodate your special needs so long as they lie within the gift of the company and you present them clearly:*

When I was let go for absenteeism, I actually felt relieved. For the past several months I had been recovering from spinal surgery that in theory was going to solve all my back problems. Theory's a wonderful thing, except when it departs from reality. I was in more pain after the surgery than before. I think my boss did her best to be understanding, and I appreciate that it wasn't easy for her, either. Some days I couldn't even get out of bed, and I'd call in sick at times when I knew they really needed me. I know all about the laws for people with disabilities—I had consulted an attorney about a year before, so I knew about my rights. But I also understood what the company did and didn't have to

*(continued)*

do about legal accommodation, and they did their fair share. So I asked that my departure date be extended by a medical leave of absence and that my separation pay include medical coverage for another six months before I would have to go on COBRA. I believe that they were willing to do all they could for me. My plan is to stay home for a while before I find another job, because I can't commit to a full schedule at this time. I'm grateful that my boss made it possible for me to take the time to recover without forcing the full burden of medical expenses on me.

—Sandra, programmer, age 34

See chapter 4 for a step-by-step method for assessing your financial situation quickly and logically.

## Start Your Documentation of the Events and Any Violations

If you believe you've been the victim of an unlawful or unfair action on the part of your employer, take notes. Even if you're not sure that the words said or the actions taken were unlawful, keep a good record of what was said and done. Try to quote as exactly as you can the words that were said. Even if the language or the behavior is graphic and offensive, quote the words and describe the actions clearly. Note the time, place, and names of other individuals present.

Taking notes at the time of the event is inappropriate or impractical, so write up your notes as soon as possible after the event. If there were others present, ask them to recount the event for you in writing, signed and dated. If they are unwilling to put it in writing, make notes on what they told you, and sign and date those notes for your file.

☞ If you are alone when the objectionable behavior occurred, in addition to making notes tell someone else the story. The assumption is that if something dramatic occurs, it is human nature to confide it to someone else. Choose a trustworthy confidant.

## Notes from the Firing Line

*If you have no other way to document abusive or threatening behavior, be sure to tell reliable people about each instance. When push comes to shove, their word can make your case for you:*

When I began working for Ted, everyone told me to watch out. But the first couple of months were fine. Ted knew a ton about the business, and I felt as if I were making an important contribution. However, one day before a long weekend, we were talking about our plans. Ted knew I had a boyfriend, and he joked that my boyfriend would get no work done around the house all weekend if I was wearing a tight sweater. I thought it was a stupid remark at the time, and I didn't give it a lot of thought. But from then on, Ted didn't let a day go by without making some personal comment. "Oh, your hair looks so pretty; I'll bet your boyfriend loves to touch it." "What are you wearing under that dress, is it stockings or panty hose?" "You're so tiny. I'll bet you don't even weigh a hundred pounds." Each time it happened, I told my girlfriends about it and they never failed to remind me that they'd told me so. Then it started to get really bad. He would always be touching me or standing around my desk, leaning over me. What finally made me crazy was the phone calls at night. He'd whisper to me, "Little lady, you don't know how powerful I am. If I want you fired, you're gone." I couldn't stand it anymore, so I went to the human resources department. They said they'd do an investigation, but it came down to Ted's word against mine, since he hadn't been stupid enough to say that stuff around other people.

Just when I thought I was going to get fired, a lawyer who worked for the company suggested that I ask my friends who I had been telling about Ted's behavior to speak to human resources. My girlfriends were great. Even though they thought we might all end up at Unemployment, they retold what I had told them to human resources. Most of them couldn't pinpoint exact dates, but people would remember that I had seemed upset

*(continued)*

after our summer company picnic, or that I had said something
on the day that a friend had to leave early to take her son to
the doctor. At the end of the investigation, it wasn't Ted's word
against mine, it was my word and all my friends' words against
Ted. Ted was forced to write me a letter of apology, and they
moved him to another job where he doesn't supervise anyone.
I didn't want to see him fired; I only wanted the harassment to
stop.

—Bernadette, administrative assistant, age 27

Information about similar events in which other people were
harmed is always useful to establish a trend. So is information about
people who were benefited unfairly, in contrast to employees who
were treated badly. If you learn of other inappropriate or unusual
events, make notes on them as well.

## Consider Reviewing Your Situation
## with a Labor Lawyer

All attorneys may look the same to you, but there are areas of concentration in the profession. This is not the time to save money
by hiring your tennis partner who concentrates on environmental
law. Even if you intend to negotiate on your own behalf, you
may want advice from someone who remains invisible but is familiar with labor/employment law. Your first objective is to negotiate
to win without resorting to a court or a government agency. If, however, your negotiations are unsuccessful and the legal aspects are
promising, you may want the attorney to continue negotiations on
your behalf, or to bring an action against your employer. (Consult chapter 5 on employment law to understand the recourse available to you.)

☞ Lawyers say they operate most effectively when they are consulted early enough to set the strategy and call the tactical plays.
Your goal is not to make this any harder on yourself than it need
be. Don't let embarrassment or shame about your behavior pre-
vent you from getting the objective advice you need.

## Notes from the Firing Line

*Embarrassment and shame about your behavior can blur your thinking. That's when professional counsel is most critical:*

A lot of my trips involved trade shows, and the partying at those events was nonstop. There were a lot of trade shows and a lot of women. And there was never a problem—until my assistant joined me. She was smart and nice-looking, so when I was asked to do a big presentation out of town, I invited her to come with me to coordinate things. We had been working late in my hotel room one night and, well, one thing led to another, and we ended being intimate. If you had asked me at the time, I would have said that she initiated it. This went on for a number of weeks, but it was becoming too much for me, so I told her that we needed to back things off. The next thing I know, I'm sitting with my boss and the company's attorney, and they're telling me that they've talked my assistant out of filing a rape charge. I was blown away. I wasn't even allowed to go back to my office and pack my stuff; I was told it would be shipped to me.

A few months went by. I found another job—nowhere near as good as my last job, but at least it was work. Then I got a letter from my company asking me how I wanted my profit-sharing program paid to me. I took the letter to my accountant, since I couldn't make heads or tails of what the company was saying. My accountant, who had been my roommate in college, is a good friend. I had never told him the story of what happened when I was fired from my job, but I told him then. When I added a PS about what a sentimental jerk I was for keeping the love letters my secretary wrote me, he practically exploded. He said I was a total fool. I had all the proof I needed to vindicate myself, yet I had meekly accepted the company's firing me. I should have fought back. But I couldn't—it was just too embarrassing.

—Allen, distributor, age 47

To minimize legal costs and streamline the process, obtain copies of as many of the following documents as you can before you meet with an attorney:

- Your employment application, written job offer, or employment contract
- Your compensation history and relevant details about how others were paid, to establish that you were treated either better or worse
- Your personnel file
- Your official job descriptions for all of the positions you held, with your annotations correcting descriptions that didn't reflect reality
- Your performance evaluations—both warnings and notes of praise
- Written communications about your termination or a group's termination
- Your separation release given to you by your employer
- Your employee handbook, applicable provisions from a supervisory manual, notes from training programs, memos, and other written communications
- Benefits information for the company and for you personally
- Correspondence you've had with any government agency relating to your dismissal, along with your notes from those conversations
- Evidence of your company's unlawful acts or wrongdoing, and the names of potential witnesses
- Notes or summaries from any meetings or summaries of discussions with your employer relating to your dismissal.

☞ Plan ahead. After you leave your employer's premises, things disappear or work rules make it difficult for certain documents to be copied. Remember, documents relating to your employment are easier to lay your hands on *before* you clear out of your office. And under the terms of the release you may be asked to sign, it's likely you'll be required to relinquish copies of proprietary material.

## Start Your Job Search

There's an old saying, "Finding a job is easier when you've already got one." This advice may not be up-to-date, given the number of layoffs over the past several years. People who would've retired with a gold watch in a prior era are now sitting in outplacement offices, trying to get their careers back on track.

Getting terminated is no longer a stigma on your employment record, and the chances that your termination will be ignored by

---

## Notes from the Firing Line

*Pay attention to unconventional job opportunities, the kind you might have dismissed without a second thought in the past. You might find something hopeful for your future:*

I was working for a company that I had mixed feelings about for lots of reasons. I stayed because my job was interesting and I didn't really have a better idea of what I wanted to do with my life. The business I was working in was sold to another company, headquartered back East. Different mind-set, different culture, different values. My job became less creative and more admin- istrative in nature. I wasn't thrilled, but I was still showing up for work. Then I got a call from an old friend who had been a baker and was writing cookbooks. She had developed a line of prod- ucts that she wanted to sell through food catalogues, and needed someone to run the business. Not a stretch for me, given my background, and much more interesting than what I was doing currently. I told her I'd think about it. Then I sat back and exam- ined my world. Because of the buyout, the new company had two people for every job. Plus there were several people who reported to me who could assume my role, given the shift of re- sponsibilities. I went to my boss, told him what I was thinking, and asked whether he'd terminate me with severance. Based upon my tenure, I'd get close to a year's pay. I said to myself, "It's now or never. If, in a year, you find that it isn't working, you can al- ways get another nine-to-five job with some company. Maybe the salary won't be the highest you've ever earned, but you'll always be employable." That's what I did. It's been two years now since I stopped wearing a tie to work every day, and I can say proudly that I've never looked back with any kind of regret.

—Keith, manager, age 53

your next employer are greatly improved. However, you will be competing with many competent people out there, blissfully unstigmatized. You should make an effort to jump-start the employment process early on, so that when you begin looking in earnest, you've already begun to build a network. You should also have the process of writing your resume and working with executive recruiters underway.

## Control the Timing

In general, the longer you remain at work before your employer tells you to pack your desk, the better it is for you—you take home more paychecks. And if the networking you've done outside of your company pays off quickly, you may enter the winner's circle: You're terminated, receive a separation package, join a new employer, and bank a large check. This may sound like a fantasy, but it can happen (and has for many lucky people).

Sometimes, timing your departure also means anticipating your eventual termination by asking to be terminated at a time convenient for you. Remember, if you're terminated and you take another job, but you leave before you conclude negotiations on your separation package, you cast doubt on the argument that you've been damaged. The company can then contend that only the minimum separation package is due. You may need to delay your start date at your new job and speed up your departure.

☞ The critical moment to escalate the termination process is when you fear that you could be swept into a mass layoff. You want to cut your own deal, unfettered by company protests that exceptions can't be made to the separation package devised for the hordes. It's easier to get an individual package when the company is not constrained by issues of "group equity."

Now is the time to objectively examine your emotional state and prepare for the next steps. Once you are officially told that you are terminated, the real work begins: negotiating your separation package. While the old adage that "a lawyer who represents himself has a fool for a client" may be true in court, it is not applicable here. It would be counterproductive at this point for someone other than you to begin the negotiations. Remember that you'll always do better if your attorney appears after you've exhausted your negotiating tactics. Sad to say, the stress of hanging in there may get to you. If you give up your office and turn the negotiations over to your attorney, it's harder to generate motivating concern or guilt in your boss or others who may be disposed to help you. Try to stick it out for as long as your sanity holds, and then bring in reinforcements.

Nevertheless, there is an important point to keep in mind: People who negotiate and "take it personally" get less. They aren't alert to opportunities. They argue about the worth of their prior job performance and the unfairness of the termination. And, worst mistake of all, they unnecessarily antagonize the person with whom they're negotiating. Accept that your job is gone, behave like a true professional, and act forcefully with quiet assurance.

# 3

# MEETING THE
# TERMINATOR

R emember all the advice you were given to help you shine during
your interviews for that dream job? Well, you'll find precious
little being offered if you're about to be sentenced to the netherworld
of the fired, downsized, separated, rightsized, dismissed, or terminated. It might seem that only wailing and gnashing of teeth relieve
the darkness here. Everyone agrees that getting hired is the emblem
of success, and everyone loves a hero. Getting the ax, on the other
hand, is considered a token of failure. Everyone hates a failure. In
this climate of shame, employers always seem to have the upper hand,
by default. So what can the hapless employee do when there is nowhere to go but down? Nothing but roll over and play dead? Wrong!
There's much to do.

☞ The termination meeting, the meeting when you are notified of
your dismissal, is not the end of life, but your best opportunity
to create conditions for a better future. Contrary to what most
people believe, you aren't without power at this crucial time.
Understand your employer's objectives as well as your own,
harmonize the two, and you will win.

## GET READY FOR ACTION

Let's analyze the situation from your employer's point of view. One
of your employer's objectives is to have you leave with minimal
noise. A pragmatic employer understands that there are potential le-

gal and other dangers to the company if the termination meeting is bungled. From your employer's standpoint, an ideal termination meeting should be surgically quick and clean. An employee is summoned to someone's office and told that she no longer has a job. The employee either accepts the decision silently, with head bowed, or pleads in tears for her job back, promising to do better work in the future and offering to accept a pay cut. When faced with tears and pleas, the employer, with an air of sympathetic regret, meticulously enumerates every error the employee has ever committed over the decades of employment. The employee, now subdued, reluctantly nods in agreement. The result is a termination on the employer's terms, seconded by a remorseful ex-employee. When the separation package is discussed, the employee is so embarrassed by her obvious unworthiness that she accepts what's offered, signs a release, and departs with dispatch. That, in any event, is what your employer hopes will happen.

Employers wield great emotional leverage in negotiating and terminating an employee. The result, malicious or otherwise, is that the terminated employee gets reduced to a state of childlike helplessness. If employers strive to do this intentionally, their purpose is to play on your fear, so that your response to termination will be guilt and embarrassment. As a result, you won't negotiate aggressively for yourself and your family. You'll accept what is given and you'll walk away quietly. What could be better for your employer?

If your employer is merely paternalistic, wanting to take care of you, that in turn will render you childlike and dependent. The effect will be the same: Because of your helplessness, you may not get all that you need and may deserve. Instead, you'll take what is given, offer thanks, and leave quietly. Don't let yourself be reduced to this.

## THE MEETING PLAN

Most termination meetings are not planned by employers to include any substantive input from the employee, other than his acquiescence to the conditions for his termination. In order to get something more than a pink slip from this meeting, learn as much as possible about your employer's reasons for terminating you. As your employer tells you why you've been terminated, just listen.

Next, you'll want your employer to make an initial separation offer. Don't end the discussion at this point by agreeing to the offer and signing a release. Set a date for the next meeting. This gives you time to think and assemble your forces.

---

### Notes from the Firing Line

*Sometimes a gut reaction to a sudden termination will pay off, but don't try this one at your job:*

I don't know what came over me that day. I didn't expect to be fired, and after I got the bad news, I didn't know what to do. So I actually barricaded myself in my office. I mean, I piled all the furniture up against the door. My boss threatened to call the police. I told him to get bent; I wasn't going to leave. Half an hour later I got a call from my lawyer. Obviously, my boss had decided against having me arrested immediately and instead brought in someone I could trust. My lawyer promised to speak to my boss on my behalf. The upshot was that I was allowed to keep my office during separation talks. As a strategy to hold on to my base, I have to admit my actions were a little screwy. But nobody can claim they weren't effective.

—"Barricade Bill," senior executive, age 55

---

☞ Your employer wants you to view the company's separation offer as final. You, on the other hand, will view this offer as no more than the opening round in a negotiation.

By not immediately agreeing to sign on the dotted line, you change the nature of the relationship from one in which your employer holds all the power to one in which you are more equal. This shift alone may give you the ability to improve your termination package. And, ultimately, you and your employer do share the same objective—that you leave quietly and without the need to pursue any open issues.

Obviously, a termination meeting in which the employee attempts to stand on equal footing with the person terminating him is not desirable from the company's perspective. Happily for employers, employees designated for termination are hardly ever able to flex real muscle. This is mostly due to the ambiguous or upsetting manner by which they first find out something is wrong.

---

### Notes from the Firing Line

*Even more than from a formal notification that you've been terminated, learning about your termination secondhand can be devastating:*

I reported to work one Monday to discover that the building services people had jumped the gun and replaced my name plate on the office door with that of my successor (a practice known as "janitorial notification"). I'd received no official word of my looming departure by noon, so my successor and I went out to lunch. Finally, at around 2:00 p.m., my boss found a few spare moments to speak with me. By this time I was furious because she had not even had the decency to tell me I'd been canned. Before she could open her mouth, I told her to not to bother—I'd figured it out for myself that I'd been fired. On the way out of her office I slammed the door. I guess I didn't realize my own anger at the moment, because when I slammed the door, all the pictures in her office came crashing down.

—Kathy, account executive, age 46

---

# TERMINATION MEETING RULES
# OF CONDUCT

No matter what state of mind you arrive in at your termination meeting, rally your courage and focus your thinking on the following rules of conduct:

## Termination Meeting Dos

- Do listen unemotionally.
- Do ask questions to clarify the points you don't understand.
- Do get the company's separation offer—in writing, if possible.

- Do make notes after the meeting is over.
- Do set a date for the next meeting.

## Termination Meeting Don'ts

- Don't ask for your job back.
- Don't debate your job performance.
- Don't make threats, specifically threats to sue or take the story to the press.
- Don't negotiate for separation pay.
- Don't sign anything.

### Termination Meeting Dos

There are some clear things that you want to do to make sure that you handle the termination meeting effectively.

***Do listen unemotionally.***    Really pay attention to what is being said, as though you aren't the person being discussed.

***Do ask questions to clarify the points you don't understand.***    Again, this is not the time to argue; this is a time to listen and reflect on what you're hearing. Since the reason why you're being terminated will affect how you negotiate, ask nonhostile questions to clarify issues. The reason for your termination will indicate what leverage will be most productive during your discussions about your separation package.

***Do get the company's separation offer—in writing, if possible.***
There is a negotiating maxim: "He who speaks first, loses." You'll want to hear the company's offer before you make a counterproposal. If you don't get your employer's proposal first, you run the risk of getting less than the company would have offered you at the outset. In effect, you negotiate against yourself. Guess who wins? And, as you'll see, your objective is to get people in the company talking among themselves about treating you fairly, thereby inducing them to negotiate your departure on your behalf.

Even though you'll make notes about the termination discussion following the meeting, you should always ask the company to put the separation offer in writing. If your employer refuses, repeat back to him or her what you understand you've been offered. It will stand out in everyone's mind as the summary of the company's terms.

And the less you talk, the more likely it is that your employer will say something (dare we suggest it?) dumb. When people are uncomfortable, they tend to ramble. Your employer, in an attempt to lighten a difficult situation, may say something unlawful or contradictory to the company's official position.

---

### Notes from the Firing Line

*The bad news is difficult to deliver and difficult to receive. Occasionally, an employer will take the coward's way out—with disastrous results:*

Rob had worked for the company for fifteen years when I was promoted and became his boss. My boss barely finished congratulating me on my promotion when he told me that he wanted my first official act to be to fire Rob for ineffective job performance. I knew that Rob's work during all the years with the company had been barely adequate, even on his best days. But since Rob had never been given any kind of warning, I asked that I be given a chance to work with him. I was told no. They wanted to eliminate a number of jobs quickly, since we were considerably overstaffed. So I fired him, making myself seemingly the least popular person in America. People really liked Rob, and his co-workers expressed great sympathy for him in his plight. They also let me know how angry they were with me. Everyone was upset because I hadn't given him a warning, which was the usual practice at the company. Because people were outraged at me, they told Rob to go over my head and speak with James, the person who had ordered me to fire Rob in the first place. And James, that weenie, in order to appear like a nice guy himself, told Rob he was being let go "to make room to give the newer guys a chance." This was not only a cowardly but an idiotic thing to say. Rob now believed he

*(continued)*

had been singled out because of his age (since no one had ever complained previously about his work). He hired an attorney to contest the firing on those grounds. His attorney was able to get a large settlement for Rob. Because of James, Rob was able to evidence illegal age discrimination where *none in fact existed*!

—Marshall, account executive, age 35

***Do make notes after the meeting is over.*** Make them soon after, so you'll remember as much as possible. Taking the notes during the meeting means you're not really listening; you're writing. And you're acting in a way that will threaten an insecure employer.

***Do set a date for the next meeting.*** This is crucial because it signals your employer that you're negotiating. Tell your employer that you've been given a lot to think about and you need a few days to consider your situation. Don't say more. Help your employer stay at ease by remaining calm, focused, and businesslike yourself. Try to set the date for the follow-up meeting so that it falls two or three days from the initial meeting. The idea is to give yourself enough time to prepare but not enough time for the tension to slacken and for your employer to place you lower on his priority list.

## Termination Meeting Don'ts

***Don't ask for your job back.*** Your primary goal in the negotiations following the termination meeting is to secure the best separation package you can. It's too late to get your job back. Don't waste your time trying to persuade your employer to rescind the termination; they want you gone, and you will be, sooner or later. Choose sooner.

***Don't miss your chance.*** When it's time to leave, recognize it and act accordingly. If, against all advice, you manage to persuade your employer to give you another chance or another job, your corporate life expectancy will be short, and possibilities for further negotiation virtually nil.

***Don't debate your job performance.*** Defending your job performance only validates your employer's right to denigrate it. There are

---

### Notes from the Firing Line

*If you can read the handwriting on the wall, don't ignore it:*

I was working in an area that had been reengineered when my boss took me aside to tell me that my job was in jeopardy. "Handwriting-on-the-wall time," he called it. Then he waved a good severance package in my face and asked me if I wanted to think it over. I said I would. When I talked it over with my family, they all agreed that I had been with this company a long time and I wouldn't want to start over at someplace new. So, I said no, I'd take my chances. The layoffs continued and a lot of people I knew left. Since what makes a company feel like your home is the people, the more friends who left, the more I regretted my choice. Then my employer reduced the company's severance policy, and my job was officially eliminated. There wasn't going to be any negotiation this time. I found an attorney and asked him if this was possible, if this was lawful. He said that there was no law that required the company to offer severance and I was hard out of luck. The most I could hope for was to point to my years of service and ask for the company to behave honorably. By this time the executive who had offered me the first severance package was long gone; guess he had seen the handwriting on the wall, too—more clearly than me.

—Brad, manufacturing supervisor, age 58

---

two specifically ill-advised reasons to debate your job performance with the person who is terminating you: One, you believe that engaging in the debate will help you retain your job. (It won't.) Two, you believe that it's "important to set the record straight." This bestows on your employer the power to set the record in the first place. Without getting into a long discussion about self-actualization, we'll say that the only record that counts is the one you keep between your ears. You know whether you were operating at full capacity or whether you had a little or a lot of room for improvement. (Incidentally, if you look hard and long at *anyone's* job performance, you'll see there's room for improvement. Don't berate yourself about the past. If you wish, resolve to do better in the future.)

Equally important, don't concede any performance deficiencies.

Everything you say can and will be held against you. You don't need to justify yourself, claiming job performance perfection. Nor do you need to delegate blame by covering up or falsifying what may have happened. And in any case, you don't have to confess your sins in order to receive absolution. This is the wrong forum for that sort of thing. At this point, just listen carefully.

***Don't make threats, specifically threats to take the story to the press or to sue.***    Your objective at the termination meeting is to set the stage for a very serious and mature negotiation to follow. Any excess of emotion will run counter to the impression you need to establish. The message you want to convey is that you are a serious force with which to be reckoned. Obviously, hollow threats delivered in shrill tones will only set the dialogue back to your third-grade playground. And your employer's thinking is that someone who is really going to sue or go to the press will do so directly, without unnecessary melodrama. You want your employer to view you as a doer, not a dreamer. Making hollow threats won't generate respect.

The exceptions to the rule about making threats of public disclosure involve two public relations nightmares—whistle-blowing and sexual harassment. If you've been a whistle-blower (someone who is aware of and has reported a major legal violation), and you believe your termination is a consequence of your actions, you may need an attorney to negotiate on your behalf. Many labor lawyers advise whistle-blowers not to negotiate on their own. The company will be concerned that during the process of negotiating the separation package, the whistle-blower may learn even more about the wrongdoing. Instead of helping you reach a swift deal with your employer, it may cause them to refuse to meet with you for fear of further disclosures. Your attorney is held to a higher standard of confidentiality than you. He can engage in conversations about the company's wrongdoing without your employer fearing the discussion will result in harmful admissions.

☞ A circumstance in which threats to go to the press are useful is a situation involving sexual harassment or misconduct. A threat to go to the press may scare a harasser out of his pants (so to speak). If the person accused of misconduct is married, often he or she is more concerned about a spouse learning of the offensive behavior than of an employer hearing about it. In morals issues, the harasser may have to answer to a higher authority than the

## Notes from the Firing Line

*If you're aware of a major legal violation on the company's part that is being covered up by your termination, then by all means be a whistle-blower. But be sure what you're reporting is the real thing:*

An old friend asked me to review her termination from the company that had employed her for over ten years. She told me she thought her termination unlawful because it followed hard upon the heels of a phone call she had made to the president of the company. She was, she assured me, a whistle-blower. This gave me pause. I had to think about it for a while, because in all of my years of law practice, I'd never represented a whistle-blower. I asked, "Did you call the president of your company to tell him about unlawful activity that you discovered your company was engaged in?"

"No," she said.

"Oh. Well," I responded, "did you call the president of your company to tell him of unscrupulous and unethical practices engaged in by your company?"

"No," she said.

"To tell him of improper and unconscionable deeds?"

"No."

"Violations of the public trust?"

"No."

"Nefarious schemes and disreputable conduct?"

"No."

"Fraud and corruption?"

"No."

"Dishonest, deceitful, vile, depraved, and treacherous acts?"

"No."

This was beginning to frustrate me. "What, then," I beseeched her, "did you call to tell the president of your company?"

"I called to let him know that his company was being run by mindless, spineless fools who had no right to be in positions of authority at this or any other place."

"Ah," I replied sadly, "if that was all it took to be a whistle-blower, we'd all be one at some point during our careers."

—Joel, attorney, age 50

company. The company will then be pressured by both you and your harasser to settle the matter quickly. This is a classic example of unity of objectives. Bring this up at the meeting *following* the termination meeting.

The same thinking applies to threats of litigation. Your employer knows that people bring suit all the time in cases that are dismissed out of hand by the courts. Anyone can and does hire a lawyer, and it's a given that your lawyer will be confident you have a good case, otherwise he or she wouldn't agree to represent you in the first place. Your threat to sue a company that probably has a number of cases pending against it already is just one more of the same. Forget the threat—introduce your legal concerns when they are most useful and appropriate.

***Don't negotiate for separation pay.***   Even if you think their offer is great and you want to accept it on the spot, don't. You aren't at your best during a termination discussion (it would be weird if you were), so don't ask more of your judgment than can be reasonably expected from it. Often, you aren't getting all you need simply because some employers hold back a little extra something. The thinking is that you will try to improve upon the package, and your employer wants to have something small to give back as a gesture of good-faith bargaining. Equally possible is that given the stress of a termination meeting, the offer, when reviewed critically by you in more temperate light of another day, may lack certain small or even large elements.

***Don't sign anything.***   For the same reason that we recommend not accepting the company's separation package at the termination meeting, we also recommend that you not sign anything. You need the time and space to reflect on the document they're asking you to sign. If it's a release, you'll want to review it with an adviser. If it's an admission of wrongdoing, you'll really want to review it with an adviser. If the company is insistent that you sign something at this meeting, act as if you smell a rat—because you do. There's no offer that could be made to you that fair dealing won't permit you to review in a thoughtful fashion. Just say no. And take a copy of the document with you to review under calmer circumstances.

Before you leave the termination meeting make sure you've accomplished three things:

1. You've clearly understood and can articulate your employer's reasons for terminating you.
2. You've been given their separation offer, ideally in writing.
3. You've set a date for the next meeting.

Remember, at this stage your employer expects anger and emotion. Your objective is to do the opposite of what is expected. Surprise your employer. If you need to come on strong, there's plenty of opportunity to do so later if things don't work out. Think about getting what you really want—a first-class ticket out of there.

# PART TWO

# PREPARING TO NEGOTIATE

# 4

# CALCULATING WHAT YOU NEED

Just as few of us want to think about the dark moment of losing a job, few professional financial planners (who should know better) have given much thought to the needs of someone who must endure a protracted period of diminished income while looking for work. The usual counsel of financial planners hasn't changed for twenty years. You'll be told, "Three-to-six months' expenses in a savings or money market account ought to tide you over in the event of an emergency." This just won't cut it today.

☞ A three- to six-months' cash hoard in the piggy bank will be stretched severely by the expenses of a job search as well as by increased health, life, and disability insurance premiums. In addition, take a hard look at your wardrobe—you'll need to replace those frayed suits, shirts, and blouses if you want to look good and radiate confidence at a job interview.

---

### Notes from the Firing Line

*The old financial rule of thumb that tells you you'll need three to six months' worth of savings to tide you over between jobs no longer works:*

When I was laid off by my company with the standard severance package for someone of my tenure—about thirty-four weeks of salary—I was planning on banking my so-called windfall. I'd

*(continued)*

---

always been sort of a "golden boy," given great assignments and good promotions. I estimated that with my contacts in the packaging industry, someone would snap me up in a week, two weeks tops.

Now, nine months later, my severance is long gone. Why? My commute to outplacement services is longer and more costly than my commute to work was; my insurance premiums, which I have maintained under COBRA, are about $600 more per month than they were through payroll deduction; rather than spending most of my time in company meetings or on company trips, where I often got a host of free meals, I'm paying for my own Big Mac. A few hundred dollars a month in carfare and food over what I'd planned is a few hundred too much. To make matters worse, my adjustable-rate mortgage on my home just went up 2 percent, increasing my monthly payments $360 per month. On top of this, my problems are compounded because thirty-four weeks of salary represents only a small fraction of the total compensation I used to receive. The rest—about 50 percent of it— was paid in bonuses. I'm in deep trouble in a way I never expected to be.

—Tom, packaging executive, age 48

Under most company's severance policies, the number of weeks' pay offered as severance is computed on base salary alone. This figure might seem adequate at first glance. However, if you've enjoyed a lifestyle buttressed by bonuses, commissions, or an override, your actual severance pay, which won't include these things, will bring you back to reality fast.

## THE EIGHT-STEP STRATEGY

When financial planners help clients devise strategies for retirement, education funding, or estate and tax planning, they employ a classic five-step process: (1) define your objectives, (2) identify the resources you have, (3) quantify the gap between your resources and your objectives, (4) take steps to close the gap, and (5) monitor your progress. This same process, enhanced by three additional steps, can be of enormous help in planning how you'll negotiate your separation package and in determining how to put the resulting funds to best use.

Here's the revised process (with additional steps in italics):

## Preparing for Negotiations

1. *Establish a budget of monthly expenses.*
2. Define your objectives.
3. Identify the resources you have.
4. Quantify the gap between your resources and your objectives.
5. *Negotiate to close the gap.*

## After Initial Negotiations

6. Take steps to close the postnegotiation gap.
7. Monitor your progress.
8. *Go back and negotiate for more if you need it.*

# PREPARING FOR NEGOTIATIONS

## Step 1: Establish a Budget of Monthly Expenses

Below is a worksheet for your first pass at a monthly budget. But before filling it out, take a few items into consideration: The most reliable source of data for completing this worksheet will be your checkbook register. For monthly expenses, use the last three months and take an average. Be sure to backtrack for the full year to pick up quarterly, semiannual, and annual payments, such as property taxes and insurance premiums.

The sad truth is, there are not a lot of things you can cut back just because you're out of work, or soon will be. In fact, when you review your worksheet, you may find that certain expenses have gone up, particularly if you've relied on your employer for benefits such as a car, professional association dues or club memberships, subscriptions, and various insurance coverages. Bear all of these in mind during your negotiations with your employer.

| Expense | Projected Cost | Current Month Actual |
|---|---|---|
| Rent/mortgage | $ | $ |
| Maintenance/common charges | $ | $ |
| Property/school taxes | $ | $ |
| Gas/electric/water | $ | $ |
| Automobiles | $ | $ |
| Automobile Insurance | $ | $ |
| Food/hygiene products | $ | $ |
| Entertainment | $ | $ |
| Tuition | $ | $ |
| Gasoline | $ | $ |
| Transportation/automobile expenses/parking | $ | $ |
| Life insurance premiums | $ | $ |
| Disability insurance premiums | $ | $ |
| Health insurance premiums | $ | $ |
| Other insurance premiums | $ | $ |
| Credit cards | $ | $ |
| Medical expenses | $ | $ |
| Membership dues | $ | $ |
| Subscriptions and publications | $ | $ |
| Cable television | $ | $ |
| Telephones (home, cellular, car, fax) | $ | $ |
| Clothing/accessories | $ | $ |
| Dry cleaning | $ | $ |
| Other | $ | $ |
| TOTAL | $ | $ |

## Step 2: Define Your Objectives

Now that you've calculated what you need to get by, define your objectives. For most financial planning objectives, this is a process requiring some quiet, serious thought. If you were planning for retirement, for example, you'd decide to retire at age sixty-five, move to a warm climate, own a home, travel a little, play some golf or tennis, and generate about 50 percent of your current gross income per year in after-tax income. You'd add up your pension and retirement plan benefits, Social Security, investments, and cash resources, calculate how much more you'd need to save, and get on with it. Your premature unemployment, however, forces you to contemplate a muddier picture.

The first question to ask is *"How long will I be unemployed?"* Or, in other words, *"How long must I plan on providing myself with a weekly income, since my employer has or will soon cease to do so?"* In the past, the rule of thumb was to assume it would take one month to find a job for every $10,000 you wanted or expected to earn. Unfortunately, you can no longer count on this rule being valid.

A widely esteemed financial-planning guru once said that the only thing a financial planner can count on is that his or her assumptions will be wrong, and that the further out the plan is projected, the more wrong the numbers will likely get. In order for your plans to hit closer to the mark, consider the job market as a pyramid. The lower on the pyramid you are (meaning the more junior), the greater the number of available jobs and opportunities. The higher you are, the fewer the available jobs and opportunities. For every hundred telemarketers, there may be only five to ten supervisory positions, and two or three who manage those supervisors. And there is only one seat reserved for the director of marketing. If that's the job you're looking for, it's likely to take you longer to find it than if you were looking for a position as a junior telemarketer. There are, of course, exceptions.

Your best-case scenario should be to land a job in three months; the worst case, one year. Fortunately, because of this pyramid concept, many companies provide their senior people with more generous severance pay. So read the fine print of the severance summary plan description.

Once you've made an assumption about how long you might be unemployed, the next question to ask yourself is *"What do I want to do now?"* Throughout the 1980s and 1990s, many laid-off workers, particularly white-collar workers, said farewell to corporate America altogether. They started their own businesses as consultants, service providers, manufacturers. If you've been thinking about a change, now may be the time. Your company may be your best source of startup capital.

---

### Notes from the Firing Line

*Alternatives to your present career are not limited to doing the same old thing. Termination gives you the chance to reassess your future:*

I had been with my company for fourteen years when the market crashed. Along with a number of other people, I was offered a voluntary separation arrangement. I couldn't help but think that if I turned it down, the next offer might be less generous and certainly less voluntary. So I accepted, took my check, packed my bags, and moved to Vermont. Today, I'm happy doing what I do best.

—Gary, ski instructor, age 46

---

If you're starting your own business, decide what you're going to do and how much capital you'll need to get started, including money to live on for a year. Start to look for a job only if, after a year, your business isn't moving in the direction you want. Remember, most businesses take two years to really get off the ground. The same rules apply to changing careers or going back to school. Do it immediately upon banking your separation package, and don't waste time. When you're unemployed, time truly is money.

After you've made some assumptions about how long you will be unemployed and what type of job, if any, you want, and you know what your monthly expenses are going to be, it's a fairly simple procedure to figure out how much money you're going to need. Take your monthly expenses, revised to reflect your out-of-work status, and multiply that figure by the number of months for which you want to plan. To play it really safe, add another three months as a cushion. This is the amount of money you'll need.

## Step 3: Identify the Resources You Have

The next step is to identify the resources that will help you make ends meet during the period of your unemployment. These may be numerous or nil. Consider the following:

• *Cash on hand.* This is cash or cash equivalents you hold in savings, checking, or money market accounts. If you own CDs (certificates of deposit), depending on their maturity, you may also consider these cash on hand.

• *Unemployment.* As a rule, unless you were fired for misconduct or resigned without provocation, you'll be eligible for unemployment benefits through your state. Your employer neither provides unemployment benefits to you nor can your employer withhold them. Accordingly, don't become overly effusive if your employer tells you that you'll be eligible for unemployment—you haven't received any concession from the company, so don't negotiate away something out of gratitude. Unemployment can be an important source of cash. While it may not seem much, that $200 or $300 per week can cover a monthly mortgage payment or car payments with some money left over for gas. Don't waste any time filing for unemployment benefits, because there is usually a one-week waiting period. Unemployment is not welfare—you've funded unemployment through your taxes during all the years you've worked. Most states have dispensed with the long lines to file your weekly claim, and you can file by phone. The benefit duration is at least twenty-six weeks (and in some states, thirty-two to fifty-two weeks).

Bear in mind that the old financial-planning rule, "Make money, pay taxes," applies to unemployment benefits as well. You'll have to pay taxes next April 15 on any benefits you receive now. Unless you're sure you'll have a job and the cash to pay the taxes, it's a good idea to count on half to two-thirds of the unemployment check to help pay the bills, and hold aside the rest in an interest-bearing account until tax time. How much you should set aside depends on your individual tax situation; the higher your tax bracket, the more you should hold aside. When calculating your tax bracket, remember: if you are receiving a significant separation payment from your employer, it may well raise your bracket. Under current tax law, this, too, is taxable income.

• *Severance pay.* To determine your severance pay under your company's policy, review the severance summary plan description. Every employee is entitled to ask for and receive a copy of the plan.

• *Employee benefits.* When calculating your cash available, don't forget employee benefits that may provide you with additional resources. These include in-the-money incentive stock options or stock appreciation rights (ISOs or SARs), stock purchase plan shares, employee stock ownership plans (ESOPs), and so on. Investigate how and when you will receive these benefits. Turning the proceeds into cash can have important tax consequences. For example, one former employee's stock purchase plan enabled her to buy stock at a discount of 15 percent off the current market value. But there was a holding period of one year for her plan, when the discount was treated as ordinary income instead of capital gains in the event of the sale of the stock. As the former employee liquidated her stock to meet her needs, she instructed her stockbroker to sell the oldest shares first (first in, first out, or the FIFO method) so that she would be taxed on the profit at 28 percent, the current *capital gains* tax rate, versus 39.6 percent, the federal *income* tax rate she was subject to at the time.

• *Investments.* While not cash per se, your investment portfolio can be made liquid and turned into cash if necessary. As an initial step, review your portfolio and determine how much income, if any, it's generating right now. Be sure that the income you're counting on is reliable: If the income comes from stock dividends, do some research to be sure that the issuer has reliably paid the dividend throughout a full economic cycle. If it's from bonds, check the credit rating of the issuer to make sure it's investment grade. Since your objective is to maximize your income during the period of unemployment, consider making changes in your portfolio to make it more income oriented. Take care in doing so, by considering the tax consequences of all of your investment decisions. It won't do you any good to take a $1000 profit to create another $50 per year in annual income, since under current tax law, you might have to pay $280 in federal capital gains taxes. (See chapter 13 for information about investing your separation money.)

• *401(k) Plans/IRAs/retirement plan monies*: A first rule of advice: *Don't touch this money unless you absolutely must.* The second and third rules are the same. Why? First of all, it's growing tax deferred, which makes it better than any other investments you may have. So, it should always be the last thing you use. Second, unless you are over age fifty-nine and a half, any monies you withdraw from these plans are subject to a 10 percent penalty tax *in addition to* the usual state, city, and federal taxes you will pay. For IRA plans, there's an exception to this rule, known as "substantial equal payments," but it requires you to make roughly the same size withdrawal each year based on actuarial calculations of your life expectancy. If your financial need is great enough to use your IRA balance, it's probably going to be a good deal more than a fraction of what you've accumulated. If you're over age fifty-nine and a half, this money becomes much more attractive, but it still should be the last thing you use.

• *Home equity*: Many people have substantial equity in their homes. If you do, this is a source of income that you may not have considered. Before you take out a home equity loan or line of credit, consider these factors: How much equity do you have, how much will it cost you to get at it, and what's happening in your local real estate market?

As a rule of thumb, don't increase your mortgage if you can avoid it. If you bought your home for $150,000 and owe $75,000 on a $120,000 mortgage, don't borrow any more than the $45,000 you've already paid in, even if you think it's worth $200,000 in today's market. This rule doesn't apply if you bought your home in 1965 for $11,000 and today it's worth $600,000.

One last thought on home equity: It's better to assume a line of credit than to take a loan. That way, you only use and pay interest on what you need to get by, month to month. In fact, if you're still working but think your job may be in jeopardy, it's a good idea to apply for that line of credit right now. *Remember, banks are more disposed to extend credit to people who have jobs than people who don't.*

• *Taxation of separation payments.* Many companies will automatically tax a severance or separation payment at a 28 percent tax rate. But some don't—they'll use the rate you have on file as your usual rate, which may be considerably higher. If you want to improve your immediate cash flow, have them tax your payment at 28 percent. Beware, however, that in April, the tax person cometh, and you'd better be ready to pay up.

## Step 4: Quantify the Gap between Your Resources and Your Objectives

Sum up all of this information on a worksheet:

| Resources | Amount |
|---|---|
| Cash on hand | $ |
| Unemployment benefits | $ |
| Separation package | $ |
| Investment income or investments (one or the other but not both) | $ |
| Employee benefit proceeds | $ |
| Retirement plan proceeds* | $ |
| Home equity* | $ |
| Total | $ |

*Only if absolutely necessary.

Take the total and divide it by the number of months you've estimated you'll need before you have a new job. *This is your monthly cash in-flow figure.*

Now use this worksheet:

Cash In-flow/Month                    $_____

Cash Out-flow/Month                   $_____

(The monthly expenses, or cash out-flow, you've estimated)

*Subtract the second line from the first.*

Total                                 $_____


If you come up with a negative number, you have a gap between the reality of your objectives and your available resources. If the figure is positive, then you have a surplus, which should be set aside each month to help you stretch out your unemployment period even longer, if necessary. If you have a surplus, skip the next sections if you like, and go to Step 7. If you don't have a surplus, read on.

### Step 5: Negotiate to Close the Gap

You've done your homework, and you have the figures to back up your story. When you enter negotiations, you will be armed with a target amount of money, legitimately arrived at, that you know you'll need to live on. Since this amount will be real to you (unlike some fantasy figure you might have pulled from your hat), you'll be able to tell your story with the power of real conviction. A compelling story, backed by logic and reason, will usually get you more than anything else you might bring to the table—and that includes the threat of a lawsuit.

## AFTER THE INITIAL NEGOTIATIONS

### Step 6: Take Steps to Close
### the Postnegotiation Gap

If you still have a gap after you've done all you can to negotiate with your employer, there are still a few things you can do to close it. Go back and take another look at your budget. Are there some things you can reduce or do without? Your monthly mortgage payment might be lowered by refinancing, depending on the interest rate environment. Be sure that the cost of refinancing doesn't eat up the monthly reduction in your payment during the anticipated period of your unemployment.

☞ If you have a second home, and there's a decent rental market, don't waste any time. Rent it.

☞ If you have any credit-card debt, and you're paying interest every month, get rid of it. Use your separation pay, a home equity loan or line of credit to pay it off. The interest on the home equity debt is tax-deductible; the interest on the credit card isn't. The home equity interest rate is also likely to be half of the interest rate of your credit card.

---

### Notes from the Firing Line

*Consider using all your assets—even those you've squirreled away for personal leisure use:*

My biggest fantasy about being unemployed was that I would be hanging out in my weekend home. Then I realized if I spent my days of unemployment there, I'd be missing out on rental income that could conceivably pay the mortgage on my first house for a full year. So I rented the weekend house. Although it was hard to forget my dream about spending a summer at the beach, the rental income went a long way toward closing my financial gap. As a result, instead of interviewing as if I had a gun pressed against my head, I was able to take my time and find a good job. Maybe when I finally retire, I'll be able to surround myself with sand and water.

—Joel, insurance adjuster, age 44

---

### Step 7: Monitor Your Progress

Financial planners will tell you this is the step people always want to ignore, and it's probably the *most* important part of the process. Once you've done all the work to establish a plan of action, you must remember what the financial planning guru said: No plan is perfect; it needs to be constantly adjusted and updated. But how? And when?

The best time to check your progress is at the end of each month, when you sit down to pay the bills. Take a few minutes and review what you've spent. Take the budget worksheet on page 50 and fill in the column labeled Current Month Actual. Make note of any shortfalls or surpluses you have on specific expense lines. If you've spent more than you budgeted on a specific line item, examine it carefully. Is it an anomaly, or did you miscalculate? If you miscalculated, then review your budget to find a way to adjust for it. If you have a surplus on a line, that's terrific. You may need it to make up for a deficit elsewhere. If you're way over budget, start the whole process again and find a way to cut back. For example, take your lunch to outplacement instead of grabbing something on the street; downsize your cleaning person and gardener—clean the house and mow the lawn yourself. *Do what needs to be done to survive.* Also, take a look at chapter 12 to learn more about maximizing your cash flow. Go through this exercise every month during your unemployment.

## Step 8: Go Back Again and Negotiate for More if You Need It

Surprisingly, this last step occasionally works. The odds may be against you, but give it try.

---

### Notes from the Firing Line

*Don't hesitate to go back and negotiate for more. The worst that can happen is that they'll say no, but they might also say yes:*

I was originally given six months of outplacement services. At the end of that period, I was on my own to find a place to make my phone calls (not to mention someone to pay for them), get my typing, faxing, and copying done and my resume updated and mailed out. These things cost money, and are very important to finding a new job, and I was running out of money and time. I went back to my employer and asked for an extension on outplacement, and they gave it to me. I'm about to begin my tenth month of outplacement.

—Alex, actuary, age 45

---

It may be particularly hard to negotiate for cash from your employer several months after the termination, but you may fare better with noncash items, such as continued perks, subscriptions and publications, access to the corporate library, or secretarial help. All of these point to getting you off unemployment and off your employer's conscience. Again, the worst that can happen is that they'll say no.

If all of this doesn't get you where you need to be, there are investment strategies that you can implement immediately to help move you toward realizing your objectives. These are outlined in chapters 12 and 13, along with guidance on how to receive and invest your retirement plan and other benefit plan proceeds. While you may not have enjoyed painting this financial picture of yourself, at least now you're in control of the details.

# 5

# EMPLOYMENT LAW: LESS THAN YOU THINK

If you believe your legal rights have been violated, and you feel able to prove it, the following brief review of current U.S. labor law will help determine whether you have a legal leg to stand on. Even if you find you don't, familiarity with the law will improve your bargaining position with your employer. In your negotiations, you'll sound as though you've been thoroughly coached by your learned counsel. Your familiarity with the law will help create that positive impression.

This chapter addresses the following issues:

- Legal protections
- Forums for bringing actions
- Language for negotiations

## LEGAL PROTECTIONS

Four kinds of law may offer you partial or complete protection from wrongdoing on the part of your employer.

1. Common labor law
2. Discrimination law
3. Defamation law
4. Unjust dismissal law

☞ At the risk of oversimplifying the issue, no federal law requires employers to behave in a certain way when terminating their employees. And once having discharged someone, employers have no legal obligation to provide any kind of separation package.

Discrimination laws require employers to *refrain from discriminating on the basis of certain personal characteristics that have no relation to employees' abilities to successfully do their jobs*. As applied to termination, discrimination laws prohibit employers *from terminating someone because of* those protected personal characteristics. In addition, employers are prohibited from *defaming* an employee's reputation by making untruthful and maliciously motivated statements. They also are prohibited from *retaliating against an employee* who is engaged in a legitimate exercise of his or her rights, or aiding the government in protecting the public at large. And finally there is a small body of law that prohibits the violation of an *"implied contract"* or the *covenants of good faith and fair dealing*.

## Common Labor Law

Very little common law governs the employment/labor relationship. The good news is that you won't have a lot of law to learn; the bad news is that you as an employee won't find all that much protection afforded by what law there is. *If you don't have a legal right, you don't have a legal remedy*. Even if it's brazenly apparent your employer has shown less common sense and good business judgment in his dealings than your goldfish, there's no possibility of a legal victory if there's no prohibition against your employer's behavior.

---

### Notes from the Firing Line

*Even if your boss's primitive behavior reflects badly on his simian ancestors, there's little you can do if it's not barred by law:*

I had always admired Henry, a man reputed to be one of the most dynamic CEOs around. When he asked me to join his company, I was delighted. I quickly discovered that Henry, while respected and admired by friends and competitors outside the office, was hated and feared by those forced to endure his company for extended periods. I remember being shocked at my first client meeting when Henry suddenly leaped onto the boardroom table screaming abuse at everyone there because he'd noticed a lightbulb was missing from an overhead fixture. I recall another time when he threw a stack of folders at someone who had made a (no doubt infinitesimal) mistake. When Henry blustered into an office yelling, "Hey, you idiot," all of us would look up.

Inevitably, one angry employee couldn't stand it any longer and sued the company, claiming she had been discriminated against because of age and gender. The plaintiff subpoenaed a number of us, and because we were under oath (and, I'll admit, maybe because we wanted a little revenge), we each told horrific stories about Henry's behavior—his sarcastic remarks, his senseless assignments, his demeaning stipulations. It was obvious from our testimony that Henry had exercised his considerable power to make everyone's life miserable. But the complainant lost her case. The discrimination agency that heard her argument found that while there was no dispute about Henry being a poor excuse for a human being, the unhappy woman employee hadn't proved her case against him. The agency concluded that Henry had not singled the plaintiff out for special treatment based on her age or gender. He treated everyone badly, in equal measure. The case was dismissed.

—Howard, Chief Operating Officer, age 54

What, then, is legally protected in the common labor law arena? Unless you have an agreement with your employer, your employment is deemed to be "at will." Employment "at will" means you are employed for an indefinite period of time, and in fact may be terminated by your employer for any reason other than those that are legally protected—at any time. The allegedly equalizing aspect of this clearly unequal equation is that as an employee, you may resign from your job at any time for any reason unless you have an agreement with your employer. The agreements precluding your summary resignation or termination by your employer may be embodied in your individual employment contract, your initial hiring arrangements, or the company's employee handbook. If you are covered by a collective bargaining agreement, you may have additional rights. The agreements precluding your summary termination are governed by your state's law.

This about covers common labor law relating to terminations, unless you are a serf or an indentured servant—doubtful possibilities.

## Discrimination Law

A number of federal laws (as well as state and local laws) prohibit discrimination by employers based on an employee's personal characteristics that are unrelated to the ability to perform a job.

☞ *Discrimination* means that you are treated differently from your co-workers with respect to the terms and conditions of your employment—either you are treated worse than others, or others are treated better than you. You must be able to show that significant differences in treatment occurred.

*Protected status.* To be legally actionable, discrimination must have occurred based on protected personal characteristics. These characteristics are called the "protected classes" and include:
- Age (Age Discrimination in Employment Act of 1978; age forty and up, Older Workers Benefit Protection Act of 1991)
- Race, color, religious creed, gender (pregnancy and sexual harassment included), and national origin (Civil Rights Act of 1866, Title VII of the Civil Rights Act of 1964 as amended by the Civil Rights Act of 1991)
- Disability (The Americans with Disabilities Act of 1990)

A number of state and local laws also offer protection to other classes—for example, marital status or sexual orientation. If the *basis* for discrimination isn't attributable to membership in a legally defined protected class, it's not unlawful. For example, if your employer singles out Bulls fans for mockery but treats Rockets fans with great deference, it's not unlawful. Bulls fans aren't a protected class.

Be careful, however. Possessing legally defined characteristics doesn't in itself prove that your employer's actions were based on those characteristics. Your employer can argue that the termination was based on valid and nondiscriminatory business reasons. In the end you are entitled to damages if you can prove your employer's business reasons were a mere pretext for covering up a discriminatory purpose.

*Statistical evidence.*    Another way to analyze whether your employer's actions are based on valid business reasons is by assembling statistical evidence. Statistical evidence provides proof that a disproportionate number of people in a protected class were adversely impacted relative to their presence in the larger employee population. Employers are sensitive to statistical evidence and will make an effort to avoid censure in this area.

---

### Notes from the Firing Line

*It's not impossible that your termination may have been for entirely arbitrary reasons, such as your employer's need to produce "acceptable" statistics:*

We knew that something was up when a meeting was called of the executive committee, a dinner meeting in my boss's conference room. Heartburn City. He told us we needed to cut several million dollars of fixed expenses and one of the fastest ways to get there was a layoff. Everyone was supposed to assemble a list of names of the unlucky within the week. It didn't take me long to realize that while our employee population was 15 percent minority, the percentage of minority employees initially selected for layoff exceeded 60 percent of the total population slated for layoff. I told my boss, who called another dinner meeting. (Reach for the antacids!) We ran the numbers, but even with swaps and switches, we were still skewed to minorities representing a disproportionate segment in the group to be laid off. Just at the point when we had no more ideas, three young white men walked by the open doorway. We all looked at each other, and added their names to the list of the terminated. We ran the numbers again, and this time, no adverse impact. Meeting over. Poor guys. Talk about being in the wrong place at the wrong time!

—Dave, employee relations, age 39

In summary, to establish discrimination you must be a member of a protected class and, subjected to adverse actions by your employer because you are a member of that protected class.

Over the past seven years, the amount of compensatory awards to discrimination plaintiffs has risen steadily with a median award in excess of $200,000. However, the number of cases won by plaintiffs has declined just as steadily. This means that if you bring an action against your employer, your chance of winning is declining; but if you do prevail, your chance of recovering significant damages is increasing. The median data by type of case breaks down as follows:

| Type of Case | Median Award | Plaintiffs Who Won (%) |
|---|---|---|
| Age discrimination | $220,000 | 54 |
| Race discrimination | $148,000 | 47 |
| Sex discrimination | $107,000 | 48 |
| Disability discrimination | $100,000 | 54 |
| Pregnancy discrimination | $87,000 | 65 |
| Sexual harassment | $38,000 | 53 |

In short, most discrimination plaintiffs have about a fifty-fifty chance of winning their case once they bring it to trial. And the 50 percent who win are the fortunate few who were able to interest competent counsel in their case in the first place and could afford the cost of litigation—on an emotional as well as dollar basis. (See chapter 6.)

## Defamation Law

Defamation laws protect employees from spoken *(slander)* or written *(libel)* untruths spread to third parties that harm the employee's reputation. Often, defamation is an issue *following* a termination, during the process of giving references to prospective employers. A small group of cases is concerned with defamation in conversations between supervisors and employees at the employee's former company. An even smaller group of cases has found if the reason offered for terminating an employee is both untrue and motivated by malice, the employee's *own* disclosure to prospective employers creates "self"-defamation for which a former employer can be held liable.

Unless you learn you've been defamed prior to your departure from the company, your knowledge won't help to enhance your separation package. That's assuming you learn of the defamation at all, since most defamation is of the whispered kind. Defamation is especially virulent because it's most often confided between executives at your old and new companies. These executives understand that despite restrictive reference policies, critical information is circulated freely on a quid pro quo basis. Those doing the information trading realize that if they don't play ball when asked to give references, they'll never get good information when they need it.

☞ The truth, no matter how unpalatable or damaging, is your employer's complete defense to a claim of defamation. Your employer can say all the terrible things about you that are true without your having any sort of legal right to stop him or her.

Other defenses asserted successfully by employers include good faith (they weren't maliciously motivated and had every reason to believe that the information was true); the information did no damage so no compensation is necessary; and the "need to know" defense—the person seeking the information had a legitimate business need to secure it. This typically occurs when a prospective employer is concerned about a relatively new kind of legal liability termed "negligent hiring" or "negligent retention." These cases frequently involve the hiring of an employee with a violent past or morals history that was not disclosed by a former employer and *should have been.*

The worst aspect of a defamation case may not be proving it, but recognizing that the act of bringing it focuses publicity on something that you didn't want said out loud in the first place. Even though the defamation may be successfully litigated as untrue, the public statement of it becomes part of the hazy history that surrounds each of us. People's recollections are imprecise at best,

and it's easier to remember some juicy story than to remember
that the person went to court and was exonerated. In short, you have
to contribute to your own embarrassment in order to be rid of it.
Defamation lawsuits are unpleasant cases to bring and win—
even though the damages from these types of cases have run well
into six figures, based upon additional damages for emotional distress.

## Unjust Dismissal Law

The countervailing premise to employment "at will" is the concept
of "unjust dismissal," or "wrongful termination." No federal laws
address the concept. In the absence of a state legislature enacting
a law (as we write this, only Montana has an unjust dismissal law),
unjust dismissal law is created by state courts. Thus *there are fifty
different views on whether the legal concept even exists*. At best,
in liberal states an unjust dismissal case is hard to establish, and
it's almost impossible to get a trial in more traditional or conservative
states.

As stated previously, employment-at-will means that your employer has the right to fire you for any reason at any time, with or
without warning. In liberal and some moderate states, under one or
all of the following circumstances, unjust dismissal concepts have
curbed employers' unfettered right to fire at will:

- The termination violates an express or implied contract between
  the employer and the employee.
- The termination involves a breach of an implied promise of good
  faith and fair dealing.
- The termination appears contrary to public policy. In addition,
  some states have adopted legislation that provides exceptions to
  the employment-at-will doctrine to whistle-blowers (people who
  make public or threaten to make public the company's violations
  of law or policy).

***The termination violates an express or implied contract between
the employer and the employee.*** Employment contracts guaran-
teeing certain terms and conditions of employment are the province
of the fortunate few who are so highly valued that their employer

## State Law Approach to Unjust Dismissal

| Liberal | Moderate | Conservative |
|---------|----------|--------------|
| Alaska | Colorado | Alabama |
| Arizona | Connecticut | Arkansas |
| California | Hawaii | Delaware |
| District of Columbia | Illinois | Florida |
| Idaho | Kentucky | Georgia |
| Kansas | Minnesota | Indiana |
| Massachusetts | Nevada | Iowa |
| Michigan | New Jersey | Louisiana |
| Montana | Ohio | Maine |
| New Hampshire | Oklahoma | Maryland |
| Washington | Oregon | Mississippi |
| Wisconsin | Pennsylvania | Missouri |
| | South Carolina | Nebraska |
| | Utah | New Mexico |
| | Virginia | New York |
| | Wyoming | North Carolina |
| | | North Dakota |
| | | Rhode Island |
| | | South Dakota |
| | | Tennessee |
| | | Texas |
| | | Vermont |
| | | West Virginia |

provides a written hiring arrangement. Most people don't have a contract and can't look forward to its protections. Courts then look to employee handbooks or supervisory promises that employees interpret as implied contracts. As a result of unjust dismissal cases, it has become quite common to read at the beginning of employment documents a sentence in bold type that begins, *"XYZ Co. is an 'at will' employer, which means that your employment here is neither for a defined period of time nor for the provision of any benefit."* You'll probably never find old-fashioned terminology describing employees as "permanent" after completing a "probationary period," or promising no layoffs in the big, happy corporate family. Courts have found binding commitments in promises of orderly industrial due process in the event of a disciplinary action being taken ("Step 1; The employee *must* be given an oral warning. Step 2, the employee *must* be given a written warning. . . ."). Courts have required employers to adhere to such commitments to refrain from arbitrary terminations—which has resulted in most employee handbooks being reviewed and rewritten by those friendly guys in your company's law department. (This is why your attorney will likely ask you for a copy of the employee handbook in effect at the time you were hired along with all subsequent revisions.)

More difficult from the company's standpoint (which means more fertile from the employee's view) are *supervisory promises* made at the time of hire or expressed along the way during an employee's association with the company. Oral assurances given to applicants during the recruitment process by company officials that "the jobs around here are recession-proof" have been held to be binding when those employees were terminated abruptly, contravening what they had been promised.

In fact, the whole issue of supervisory promises is somewhat nightmarish to employers because they rely on supervisors to be the eyes and ears of the company. When a supervisor becomes the unguarded mouthpiece of the company, the person who's supposed to keep liability at bay may be the one causing it. This frequently happens for reasons not sanctioned by the corporation—such as when a supervisor tries to be a "nice guy" in the eyes of those he or she supervises, or when he or she lacks the courage to deliver a straightforward message.

## Notes from the Firing Line

*Your careful record of the promises of long-term employment made to you can come in handy:*

I was hired by Ken, a man I had known somewhat vaguely at my first job. My reputation as a hard worker must have preceded me, because when Ken went to another company, he called me and hired me almost immediately. At first I was flattered by his praise, but over time, not only was the praise too effusive for the work I was actually producing, but I began to realize that Ken really didn't have a glimmer of an idea about what I was doing or how well I was doing it. It became clear to me that Ken just wasn't technically competent and that he had hired me to cover up his own shortcomings. Eventually, Ken's boss began to notice the skill gaps in Ken, and then things started to fall apart. I was working harder than ever and doing respectable work, but after they cleared Ken out, it was evident to me that I'd be next. I guess they figured that an incompetent would surround himself with people who were equally incompetent.

All along, I had made notes about Ken's promises to me: "We'll retire at the same time and buy houses next door to each other in Florida." "All you need around here to have job security is do a good job—and you do great work." "Your stock options alone will give you enough to retire on." When I was called in to get my walking papers, I just flashed my little notebook, read a few key passages, and suddenly my departure deal was vastly improved. Maybe Ken was looking out for me in the only way he knew how.

—John, packaging engineer, age 52

***The termination involves a breach of an implied promise of good faith and fair dealing.*** This cause of action grows out of insurance law, which recognizes that the agreement between an insurer and the insured is not between equals (the insurance company has a lot more going for it by way of bargaining strength). Courts have required insurers to behave "reasonably" and "fairly" in addition to the insured's other contractual or specific rights of enforcement. On these occasions, courts have extended their authority to help those who have been victimized, even though there was no precise legal wrong. Language about *shocking the conscience of the court* crops up in these cases. Since courts usually rely on a standard considerably less nebulous than "what is fair," plaintiffs seldom win on good-faith and fair-dealing cases in the absence of other grounds, such as discrimination or a public policy issue. For example, courts have found a violation of public policy when employees have worked up to a critical date in the employment relationship and then are arbitrarily or capriciously denied a benefit or compensation that they should have earned. So, employees who were terminated on the eve of vesting in their pensions have successfully evidenced bad faith and unfair dealing.

If your attorney proceeds with this cause of action, the more you have of the following will help:

- Age and tenure
- Good performance evaluations and recognition
- Promotions and compensation
- Opportunities to leave for other employment, which you turned down
- Stable employment that you left based upon recruiting promises
- Drama associated with your termination

***The termination is contrary to public policy.***    In a number of states, laws require employers to permit employees to take time off from work to perform certain civic duties. Failure to allow this or retaliation against an employee for performing these duties may result in a court's intervention. Examples of civic duties include military reserve duties, serving on a jury, filing a workers' compensation claim, involving yourself with a union, or (and courts really frown on employer retaliation for this one) testifying against your employer. Similar protection is afforded whistle-blowers— people who report to state or federal authorities that a law has been violated (or act in good faith in making such a report, even if the law has not in fact been violated). Typically, whistle-blowers report health or safety hazards, cover-ups by their employers, or discriminatory activity.

*Think twice before taking them to court.*   Because the risk of being charged with discrimination or unjust dismissal is clear to most employers, companies are exercising increased caution in *any* termination situation. Below is a chart that one large employer gives to all its supervisors so that they will have a checklist that they can proceed through methodically before they terminate anyone.

## Getting Terminations Right the First Time

The column on the left represents the kinds of actions that employees can bring against their employer. Ask yourself all the questions in the middle column. If the answer to your question is NO, continue down the questions in the middle column. If your answer is YES, go to the column on the right to correct the process before proceeding.

| Legal Problem | Questions to Be Asked | Actions to Be Taken |
| --- | --- | --- |
| Adherence to company polices and procedures | Will this situation create an exception to company policies/ practices? **If no;** | **Correction:** Investigate issue and make decision, recognizing impact on policy/practice. |
| | If the dismissal is performance-based, does employee's performance appraisal contradict the problem? **If no:** | **Correction:** Put the employee on a formal performance counseling program. Hold decision on termination. |
| | Is the termination very abrupt? **If no:** | **Correction:** Follow published progressive discipline steps and proceed. |
| Public policy issues (whistle-blowing, retaliation) | Does termination involve external obligation of employee (jury duty, military service, family illness, religious days)? **If no:** | **Correction:** Seek advice; lean toward allowing employee to fulfill obligations. |
| | Is there a claim by | **Correction:** Review |

Getting Terminations Right the First Time *(continued)*

| Legal Problem | Questions to Be Asked | Actions to Be Taken |
|---|---|---|
| | employee of retaliation by management for behavior that was proper by employee? **If no:** | by more senior management, human resources, and law departments. |
| | Has employee filed any claim that could be associated with the termination? **If no:** | **Correction:** Review by human resources and law departments to decouple issues. |
| | Are there issues of potential concern to external community at large? **If no:** | **Correction:** Review by more senior management. |
| Wage and hour issues | Does employee claim any bonus, back pay, overtime, compensatory time, vacation, or commissions that won't be received as a result of termination? **If no:** | **Correction:** Review by human resources and law departments. |

All okay? Proceed with the termination.

So, be cautious about declaring to your employer, *"I'll see you in court!"* They'll be cautious about seeing you.

## FORUMS FOR BRINGING ACTIONS

There are three forums in which you can bring an employment law action:

1. A state, municipal, or federal human rights agency
2. A court
3. An arbitration tribunal

There are pros and cons to seeking justice in each.

## A State, Municipal, or Federal
## Human Rights Agency

Employees who believe that their employer has *discriminated* against them file a charge of discrimination with the Equal Employment Opportunity Commission (EEOC) or the human rights tribunal of their state or municipality, not a lawsuit.

☞ The difference between a charge of discrimination and a lawsuit is significant: Filing a charge is free and the agency handles the investigation free of charge. This gives the complainant an opportunity to preview the company's defense.

For employees, this provides valuable discovery because you learn how your employer will counter your assertions. At the end of the process, the agency will issue a right-to-sue letter, which gives you the ability to file a lawsuit in a court, perhaps with some sense of how strong your case is against the company. While you may wish to have your own attorney working with you during this process, at least up to the filing of the lawsuit, an attorney is, in theory, unnecessary. In reality, moving your claim along through the channels of an overburdened administrative agency may require all the help you can give it.

The downside of all this free effort on your behalf is that you often get what you pay for. The EEOC backlog is well known, and they don't have enough time or staff to do all that they might to investigate and process your charge. The state and municipal agencies are also up to their ears in work, because under most states' law, they must review all charges brought before the EEOC and either pursue them or pass them back to the EEOC. All this takes time. And your obligation to file your charge with the EEOC or your state's human rights agency is governed by strict rules. If you operate without the benefit of counsel, the deadline issues are yours to track.

## Courts

As described above, most *unjust dismissal* causes of action are tried in courts and aren't within the jurisdiction of human rights tribunals. Bringing a lawsuit in a court is expensive. But if you want a jury of your peers to hear your case, you'll need to finance the process. The expenses of litigation really start to mount during the pretrial stage of discovery, in which parties to the litigation are supposed to narrow the issues to expedite the case once you're actually in a courtroom. To do this, the attorneys can depose parties to the action and witnesses (formally ask them questions in the presence of your attorney and the attorney for the company). The plaintiff, who may have found another job, may be required to sit through hours of depositions, all in the name of rapidly ascertaining the truth. Another tactic is to attempt to bury the opposition in paper, using interrogatories, which are written questions that require a written response or the production of a document. All this time—deposing witnesses, answering interrogatories—translates into big costs.

## Arbitration Tribunals

The role of arbitration as an alternative dispute resolution process has expanded dramatically over the last several years. The arbitration tribunals are designed to provide quasiformal, inexpensive, and speedy resolution to disputes. In the past, arbitration was likely to be used by employers and unions engaged in collective bargaining disputes, construction and other industries involved in commercial disputes, and individuals who had employment contracts.

That's all changed. Today, it isn't uncommon to find that upon being hired, you must agree to arbitrate all prospective and potential disputes arising out of your employment with your brand-new employer. In so doing, you agree to relinquish all rights to bring your dispute to a human rights agency or a court. Sometimes the difficulty with arbitration is the uneven abilities of arbitrators because of their lack of experience in deciding employment cases. Sometimes the difficulty with arbitration is the speed with which a case can be brought and the less stringent rules of evidence—swift justice may not always be the best justice. However, under a company's alternative dispute resolution policy, you relinquish your choice of forum upon being hired, so the matter becomes academic. You no longer have the option of bringing your case elsewhere if you want to work with that employer. Be aware that courts have upheld employers who implement an arbitration policy and require that current employees follow it without providing additional consideration (that is, something of value in return for employees giving up their freedom of choice).

The choice of forum may not truly be a choice. If it is, your attorney should help you decide which is the right place to bring your action based on the facts of your case.

## LANGUAGE FOR NEGOTIATIONS

Attorneys have often been (correctly!) accused of speaking a foreign language in order to justify their existence. The law wasn't supposed to be obscure and confusing, but to most of us, it is. Ideally, if the foregoing has been useful to you, you've already added some new words and expressions to your vocabulary. That's what happens when you hang around with lawyers.

If you decide to engage in the process of negotiating with your employer without the benefit of counsel, you may wish to sprinkle your conversation *judiciously* with these terms:

**Cause of action**    The facts that will give a person a right of judicial redress or relief against another. ("I would prefer to negotiate an amicable settlement with the company even though I believe I have a good cause of action against you.")

**Damages**    Compensation that may be recovered in the courts by a person who has suffered loss, detriment, or injury to his person, property, or rights through an unlawful act of another. ("I've been damaged by the company's failure to live up to the commitments made to me.")

**Defamation**    An intentional false communication either published or publicly spoken that injures another's reputation or good name. ("Telling my new employer that I was fired when I quit is defamatory.")

**Discrimination**    A failure to treat all persons equally where no reasonable and relevant distinction can be found between those favored and those not favored. ("Promoting only men is discriminatory.")

**Due process**    An orderly and fair proceeding that provides safeguards for the protection of individual rights. The person should be notified that there is a proceeding against him or her, be provided an opportunity to be heard in his or her own defense, and to make an informed choice to acquiesce or contest the findings made. The remedy selected should have a reasonable and substantial relation to the objective being sought. ("I was never warned that my work was substandard. You didn't provide me with due process before you fired me.")

**Fair-dealing and good-faith covenants**    An agreement made and executed in honest belief and the absence of malice or a design to defraud or to seek unconscionable advantage. ("Firing me the day before my stock options vest shows a lack of good faith and fair dealing.")

**Implied contract**    The intention, in entering into the agreement, is not manifested by explicit and direct words, but gathered by deduction from the circumstances, the general language, or the conduct of the parties. ("Telling me this company never lays off its employees was the reason I accepted your job offer. I consider that promise to be an implied contract.")

**Oral assurances**    A spoken declaration tending to inspire trust, confidence, and belief. ("My supervisor promised me a raise if I completed the project on time. I consider that to be an oral assurance.")

**Protected class**    A group that the law seeks to protect. ("Gender and age are protected classes.")

**Public policy**    Community common sense and common conscience applied to matters of public morals, health, safety, welfare; a person's duty to other human beings. ("Firing me because I was absent while serving jury duty violates public policy.")

**Unjust dismissal**    A termination that is contrary to right and justice or the standards of conduct furnished by the laws. ("Firing me after I brought in a big client that would result in you having to pay me a large commission constitutes an unjust dismissal.")

**Whistle-blower**    An employee who refuses to engage in or reports illegal or wrongful activities of an employer or fellow employees. ("I was fired because I was a whistle-blower who had testified on behalf of colleagues who were laid off.")

Remember the advice against involving an attorney in the negotiation process before you've exhausted all the efforts that you can make on your own behalf. Employers otherwise willing to talk with you will run scared at the prospect of dealing with your attorney. And if you throw around too many legal expressions (or you use them incorrectly), you may hinder rather than help your cause.

# 6

# HIRING AN ATTORNEY

S ometimes there are things about a termination that can't be re- solved by you in negotiation. You may feel that your dismissal was predicated on illegal discrimination of some kind (see chapter 5), or negotiations that started in good faith fail, apparently without hope of resurrection. What do you do? Depending on the issue, an attorney continuing your negotiations or ultimately bringing a legal action may be the only way to resolve your situation.

Bringing an attorney into separation discussions with your employer, let alone bringing a legal action, is an enterprise that will forever change your relationship with your company. It's crucial that you now consider what you'll have to know and do in order to prevail. In this chapter we'll cover the essential issues:

- Finding the right counsel
- What it will cost you to hire counsel; the cost structure that makes the most sense for you
- The information your attorney will need
- How you can help keep fees to a minimum
- All the other pain that's in store for you if you sue

## FINDING THE RIGHT COUNSEL

Finding a competent professional is always a tough task—whether you're seeking a plumber, a heart surgeon, or an attorney. You're usually out of your element, and you have little choice but to rely on the good faith of strangers. This notwithstanding, you can still judge a promising candidate by asking yourself two questions:

1. Do I trust this person (meaning, "Does he or she appear to understand the technical aspects of the job to be done")?
2. Do I respect this person (meaning, "Do I want to go through what may be a long and possibly harrowing experience with him or her")?

While you may feel that you're not capable of rating an attorney's technical competence, your assessment of the attorney's intelligence, integrity, and ability to articulate your position should serve you well. In addition, your positive answer to the second question will at least let you hire someone you respect. In the end, you're assessing the professional's bedside manner, and that's important for your comfort and your prospects of further collaboration.

---

### Notes from the Firing Line

*In assessing the ability of an attorney you may hire, be sure that the attorney's motivation is to win your case for your sake, not for his or her own:*

When I was fired, it rippled through the company and touched everyone. People were devastated when they discovered I had been marched from the building by two security guards, as if I were Public Enemy Number One. Even the security guards were affected. One of them was practically in tears. He had been hired by me ten years before, and he couldn't believe he had been assigned to help me carry my boxes from our offices. I decided to fight the indignity and get even. Throwing the severance offer back in my employer's face, I told them, "You'll be hearing from my lawyer." The only problem was, I didn't have a lawyer.

I talked to a really aggressive attorney who sounded like he'd been around and knew it all. He made me a little uncomfortable when he bragged that after he'd gotten through with my former company, a nuclear holocaust would seem tame by comparison. But he assured me we'd make new law, and the humiliation I suffered by being escorted from the building would be the cornerstone of our action. I wasn't particularly interested in making new law; what I wanted was to win—to win big, and to win now.

I should have listened to my fears about my lawyer. Big talk,

*(continued)*

I was forced to recognize, doesn't always produce big results. When we finally brought my case to trial, it had been three years since I was fired. And I lost. The court concluded that the act of escorting someone from a building was not defamatory in the absence of other, more explicit gestures made by the security guards. If I had known that, I would have told my ally, the guy I had hired ten years before, to handcuff me. I'm certain he would have done it for me as a favor.

In hindsight, it's obvious my attorney was on the lookout for his own notoriety and not my best interests.

—Jerry, payroll manager, age 50

It might sound frivolous to suggest that an attorney you respect is the best one to handle your case. You might reason that this matches the process used to select the prom king for the high school dance. Not, you might suggest, the best method of selecting learned counsel. But if you are unable to summon the technical expertise to properly evaluate a professional, you still possess the abilities that have gotten you through countless other difficult situations, namely, common sense and good judgment about people. This is another way of taking control in a situation that may at first appear daunting.

What causes you to feel comfortable around some people quickly? Well, for one thing, you sense they're interested in you. Common sense tells you that those who are more interested in what they have to say than in what you have to tell them aren't the best candidates to work on your behalf. This is especially dangerous in an attorney, in whom you'll invest your wholehearted trust. It's not so great in a plumber, either.

Excellent attorneys are good listeners. They understand that winning cases are built on the facts of each individual's particular situation. Law, employment or otherwise, is crafted to mean what it says. For example, there's not a lot of debate as to whether Title VII of the Civil Rights Act of 1964 prohibits employers from discriminating against employees. It does. *Applying* the law to the facts of a situation is where the technical competence comes into play. The important issue is whether *you* have been discriminated against by *your* employer. A winable case isn't the result of a winning law but of winning facts. What you're looking for, then, is not the lawyer who dazzles you with legalese, but the one who is the most probing into your situation. Your work experiences, which will comprise the facts of your case, are unique. You're looking for someone who asks you revealing questions and then listens to your answers carefully. Certainly, you'll need enough information about applicable law to help your attorney gather and present the winning facts, but if the attorney recites a dizzying array of law at you when you interview him or her, it would be better if you continued your search for learned counsel elsewhere.

## Where to Look for the Right Attorney

How do you find an attorney who is an excellent listener? Word of mouth is your best bet, and a bar association reference is the final resort. Ask nonlabor attorneys for names of employment law specialists. Find plaintiffs who have secured counsel. Ask people in human resources for names of attorneys they wish never to see again.

As there are concentrations in other professions, labor lawyers concentrate, too. Some represent only plaintiffs, others represent only management, and some are pleased to represent either. Since you're looking for someone who has your best interests at heart, don't bother trying to hire lawyers who represent only management. Management attorneys, however, like human resources practitioners, can be great sources for the names of opposing counsel—counsel whom you might want to represent you—because they'll remember who has given them a tough time in the past. The highest commendation for prospective counsel you could get would be "And, I hope never see that tough character sitting opposite me again."

Bar associations will give you names of attorneys who specialize in any area of practice you request. Bar associations don't qualify the attorneys who are referred to you; it's up to you to assess their abilities and track records in their handling of similar matters. To do this, first show the list to any attorney who you respect to see if he or she recognizes any of the names. If the attorney knows something positive about any of them, then you'll need to interview the prospective attorneys yourself. Do so carefully.

## Notes from the Firing Line

*Just as you should never point a loaded gun at someone unless you intend to use it, you should never threaten to sue unless you plan to go through with it. And if you do, be sure your hired gun is powerful enough to demolish the target:*

There was a senior manager at my company who was gay and quite outspoken about his sexual preferences. A number of straight men complained that whenever they bent over the photocopying machine, John would sneak up behind and say things like, "Oh, it just makes me crazy when you do that." After consulting with our counsel and issuing several warnings to John about sexual harassment, we fired him. We knew the situation was potentially controversial, but we believed we had done the right thing. In retaliation, John quickly hired an attorney who is known as a barracuda—even the president of my company quakes when he hears her name. She was on the case for only a short time when I was handed John's revised separation and release papers to proofread. Given that we had terminated him for cause, I was amazed at the size of John's settlement. I'd recommend his attorney to anyone who wanted to strike terror in the hearts of officials at any company. Especially if they have a weak case.

—Pam, human resources, age 44

### Interviewing a Prospective Attorney

After you've had a chance to talk to a prospective labor attorney, the first step is to decide if he or she has really listened to your story. Did the attorney pick up any subtleties about your company relationships? Did he or she ask questions that uncovered issues you may not have realized were significant? The attorney would be passing a real test in your estimation if he or she could remember the names of the players in your life the first time around, without you supplying a scorecard.

After the attorney is through asking questions about your situation, it's your turn to ask some. Here are ten essential questions that will get right to the heart of the matter:

1. Do you think I have a good case against my employer? If so, or if not, why?
2. What elements of the case are not in my favor?
3. Have you handled cases that were similar to mine? Did you win or lose those cases? If you lost, what happened? Was the loss anticipated?
4. What are the alternatives to litigation?
5. What are the alternatives to litigation? (Note the repetition of this question. Ask it several times throughout your interview if the direction seems to be heading you precipitously to court.)
6. What do you propose as our next steps?
7. How long will litigation or its alternative take?
8. What role will I play in bringing this matter to a successful conclusion?
9. Whom may I speak to that will serve as a reference for you?
10. How much will it cost and how will you bill me?

With some attorneys the initial consultation may be free; with others it could cost you several hundred dollars. In any event, at the end of the discussion you may not want to proceed with the attorney, or he or she may advise you that you don't have a good case. It is possible, too, that the attorney might advise you that your case is solid, but you may be turned off to the whole process when he or she outlines the necessary next steps. (Read on.)

## THE COST OF COUNSEL

Beyond the initial consultation, attorneys charge in one of two ways: fees based on contingency or fees billed on retainer. With the former, your attorney charges you nothing unless you recover money, and then he or she takes a percentage of your court judgment or settlement from your employer. Retainer attorneys charge by the hour and will almost certainly ask for an advance against their retainer. Since employment litigation is often protracted and the judgments not large, many attorneys prefer the fee basis. In urban areas a typical employment case will *start at* $10,000 in attorney fees (in 1997 dollars). If your case goes to trial, you should anticipate the costs running much higher. If you aren't able to negotiate additional money, or if you sue and lose your case, attorney's fees are of course non-refundable.

Contingency attorneys, because they must commit a great amount of initially uncompensated time to researching and preparing, are more likely to be interested in cases that involve the potential for a class action—that is, contingency attorneys want to represent you and a large group of similarly situated people who have been fired or laid off together. Your case might also be particularly attractive if it were potentially newsworthy because of who you are or who your employer is, or if what happened to you was particularly scandalous. In this case the attorney would be writing off any uncompensated time as worthwhile advertising expenses.

☞ The attorney you select will probably not give you a choice in the matter of billing on a contingency or an hourly basis. If you have a choice, your decision needs to be made based on your cash on hand versus cash expected down the road.

If you can afford it, paying your attorney on an hourly basis means that whatever you recover is yours alone. If you anticipate a large recovery and the facts are on your side, paying your attorney at an hourly rate gives you the largest settlement. If you can't afford the fees up front, the case promises to be a tough one, and the judgment may be small compared to the satisfaction of the victory, grab at a contingency fee as soon as it's offered.

If your ability to afford counsel is not the issue, do some straightforward arithmetic. Compare fees for an attorney who charges by the hour with the fees of one who will take the case on contingency. Let's suppose you believe you can recover $50,000 as a settlement from your employer. A fee-charging attorney may want $200 an hour, with $10,000 up front as an advance against retainer. A contingency fee–charging attorney, on the other hand, will probably want 30 percent (or $15,000) of your possible $50,000, after a successful settlement. If either attorney estimates spending more than seventy-five hours on your case, a contingency fee–charging attorney is the better choice, since 75 hours × $200 per hour = $15,000, the amount of the contingency fee. If this attorney must spend more time to win your case, you will not be charged for it.

If you choose a lawyer who charges a contingency fee, the best arrangement for you would be one in which the fee was based on your attorney securing incremental monies for you. For example, your employer offers you $10,000 as a separation package before you introduce your attorney into the equation. Your attorney agrees to a fee structure that provides for a percentage of what he or she secures for you on top of that. If your attorney is then able to negotiate for an additional $5,000, the fee would be based on a percentage of $5,000, not on a percentage of the full $15,000 package.

## INFORMATION YOUR ATTORNEY WILL NEED

To maximize the process and, incidentally, minimize your attorney's costs, consult chapter 2 for a list of documents you should be sure to have available when you meet with your attorney. Obtain copies of as many of the items on the list as you can before you clear out of your office.

## KEEPING FEES TO A MINIMUM

You'll save money when you involve an attorney in your separation:

• If your attorney steps into your negotiations with your employer at an advanced point in the negotiating process, when minor elements have been arranged more or less to your satisfaction. Some employers will hold back in negotiations, waiting to see if you're really serious about making an issue out of it. (Your employer will know you're making an issue out of it when you signal so by hiring an attorney.)

• If you file your discrimination charge with the Equal Employment Opportunity Commission or your state's human rights agency. Filing a charge is free, thus the costs for seeking and perhaps obtaining redress may be less. It's also another signal to an employer that you're serious about this. You've gone to the trouble and expense of hiring counsel and filing with the EEOC, and this may prompt your employer to initiate or renew offers to settle the matter. This too, could minimize your legal expenses.

## Avoid Costly Behavior

Being unprepared, unfocused, or emotionally needy will eat up hours of time without producing any constructive return on the fees paid to your attorney. What you *refrain* from doing can help as much as—or even more so—than what you actually *do*.

***Don't replay your anger and distress beyond what is necessary.*** You'll know you're doing this if you find yourself telling and retelling your attorney how you held up your end of the argument with your employer, instead of recalling what was said to you. Here's an example of what this sounds like:

> So my boss sneers at me, "We expect you to do a good job at this presentation. And remember to keep your hormones under control." So I reply to him, "You can't speak to me that way. That's discriminatory. I'm really surprised that you would consider that to be an appropriate remark in today's work environment. My job performance has always been stellar. For you to say something so totally unrelated to my skill set and competencies . . . (blah, blah, blah)."

Too many sentences beginning with "So, I told him . . ." or its equivalent are a good tip-off that you aren't focused on the right things. Your attorney will either coach you on how to hold up your end of the conversation or become satisfied that you can do it yourself without help. Spending time repeating how you voiced your righteous indignation misses the essential element of the dialogue—the unlawful and dumb statements your employer made to you. That's what your attorney needs to hear, because your case is built on your employer's errors, not on your wit and wisdom. Realize that by focusing on yourself at that meeting, you may not remember some winning gem uttered by your employer. If replaying your side of the conversation is cathartic for you, find someone who isn't charging you premium rates to listen. Or if you're interested in paying premium rates for someone to listen to your anger and pain, let it be to a professional counselor who is trained to help you recover from a very upsetting experience.

***Don't believe that your attorney will be intrigued by surprise revelations.*** ("Oh, by the way," you whisper as you walk into court, "we're going to win this one. I've been sleeping with my boss!") Don't believe that the embarrassment you feel about your errors and omissions will abate ("I didn't know how to tell you this before," you confess as your attorney begins to turn the full power of his blazing negotiating skills on your boss. "But I've been pilfering a little bit of money from the company treasury over the years, and I think somebody may be suspicious.").

☞ Waiting too long to confess your misdeeds to counsel is, in itself, a misdeed. Your attorney is paid by you to take the facts of your situation and organize them into a winning case—*all* the facts, even ones that cast you in a less than desirable light. Did you make mistakes at your job? Everyone does, and you don't have to be perfect to prevail. You do, however, have to be candid with counsel. Let your attorney earn his or her fees by figuring out how to best help you. Warts and all.

***Don't have your attorney organize the files, notes, pay stubs, other data of your case.*** This error can do most damage at two key moments: first, when you're trying to secure counsel; second, when you're preparing your case. The first can be fatal, because you'll be unlikely to secure the best counsel available if you can't coherently outline your facts. Good lawyers won't have time to go through your manila folder containing the cryptic notes you made during the last fifteen years about your employer's callous, insensitive behavior. You won't be taken seriously, despite the fact that you may have been seriously wronged. In the second case, having hired counsel, it's more productive and cost effective for you to go through the shoebox that contains the record of the compensation paid to you over the past decade.

# THE PAIN IN STORE FOR
# YOU IF YOU SUE

Hiring an attorney and pursuing a legal solution to your termination may be the only recourse you have to attain a just settlement. But if you rush enthusiastically along this path, and you haven't considered all the consequences of your journey, you may end up a loser. Here are some caveats you should consider:

• Of those situations in our lives that bruise us, the most vexing are the ones that continue hurting long after the initial painful incident is over. A lawsuit, no matter how just and necessary, is guaranteed to imprison you in the pain of the past by keeping it alive, fresh, and current. Instead of being able to let the dead past bury its dead, you as the plaintiff in a litigation will be condemned to relive the dreadful moment. Sometimes, because of delays, your day in court will not arrive until years after the event occurred. This means that your memories, documents, and the memories of your witnesses must be preserved. In short, if you've been longing to carry an overwhelming amount of emotional baggage around with you, litigation will just do the trick.

• If you hadn't been feeling rotten enough because of this difficult event lingering like a winter cold in summer, your employer's counsel is prepared to make a bad situation even worse. Imagine for a moment the embarrassment of having to explain to your attorney clearly and without excuse your humiliation at the hands of your employer, or having to explain what a fool you made of yourself at work. Now, imagine yourself in public, in open court, repeating the same sorrowful things. Next, imagine being cross-examined by your employer's counsel who, you can be sure, will not stop at your version of things. He or she will surely have discovered some surprising facts or will make some highly embarrassing allegations you've never considered. While it is your attorney's job to protect you from distorted facts and false allegations, you're the one who's bound to emerge with a red face. Based on the "deep pockets" theory of law ("Sue only defendants who have pockets filled with enough money to make your case worthwhile"), your employer will certainly be more experienced at getting sued than you are at suing, and probably has greater financial reserves to pursue a protracted legal action. Your employer may even regard lawsuits as a normal risk of doing business. It's no sweat for the company to spend "the usual" cost to mount a defense.

---

### Notes from the Firing Line

*People win lawsuits overwhelmingly for reasons other than simple Truth, Justice, or the American Way:*

When I started practicing law, I worked for a sole practitioner named Mike. In my naïve and unsophisticated sense of things, Mike was Perry Mason and Clarence Darrow rolled into one. In truth, I still believe he's a great attorney. Several years after I left his office, I had moved on to the law department of a Fortune 100 company. It happened that an employee we fired decided that she had been discriminated against because of her age. She showed up with my old boss, Mike, in tow. I hadn't seen Mike in years, and it was great catching up. He was just as I remembered him: smart, incisive, and thoroughly prepared. But so was I. And unlike Mike, I had a big law department behind me with large amounts of money at my disposal. When we went into discovery, I buried Mike in paper. Every step of the way, I did exactly what the system allows: I made it as difficult as possible for the other side to win. Finally, after more than a year, we settled. The plaintiff did okay—it was a fair settlement. But she wouldn't have gotten even that if she hadn't hired someone as good as Mike. The real victory was mine, however, and I won based on the weight of the evidence—and by weight I mean tonnage. No matter how good one lawyer is in the courtroom, and no matter how well prepared the case, a table full of opposing lawyers with great preparation and plenty of money always counts heavily toward the outcome of a case—and often determines it.

—Glen, attorney, age 51

---

•   Your expectations of privacy will be adversely affected. Not only does your company have access and control over all the records that you will need to find, they also have access to your former management and co-workers. Your case may depend on employees still employed by the company. The leverage a company can exert against people who still work there is considerable. On the other hand, they may not need leverage to turn on you, since people who sue are branded traitors in many corporate cultures. Don't be surprised if your ex-colleagues volunteer to testify in their company's cause. Sadly for you, they may have decided that their personal agendas come first, even before the righteousness of your case. Did you get a promotion someone else wanted? Did you reprimand a subordinate for doing a poor job? Well, it's payback time. You may be shocked that your perfectly clear recollection of the past in no way squares with the recollections of others who viewed the same events. This is a time when no good deed goes unpunished.

• Despite assurances that your job performance need not have been absolute perfection in order for you to prevail in negotiating an increase to your separation package, once you begin a lawsuit, you should be prepared to hear about every one of your perceived faults and flaws. Be prepared to hear them in great detail. This recitation of faults and flaws won't be restricted to those occurring within the four walls of your office. Within the bounds of relevance, any information that sheds light on your job performance or corroborates the company's business reasons for terminating you can and will be treated as fair game. As with politicians who enter public life to discover that the ghosts and shadows of their pasts have become a part of the general domain, so you should be prepared for scrutiny—scrutiny that will extend into both your public and your private lives.

## Notes from the Firing Line

*Be prepared to be judged on your personal life as well as your professional one:*

I was let go as part of a big layoff on a trading floor. Everyone knows that Wall Street is cyclical business, so I took my separation package and started to look for a new job. A few months later, I heard that a couple of folks who worked with me had been contacted by my company and told that there were jobs available. When I called my ex-boss, instead of welcoming me back with open arms, he seemed edgy. After several conversations, it became clear to me that the company was discriminating against me because of my race. So I sued. Someone tipped me off that I was regarded as "an attendance problem," but my attorney told me not to be concerned, because I had never been given any kind of written warning. The next thing I know, the company is asking for copies of my driving record and interviewing my neighbors about my drinking and drug use. Wall Street is known as a jungle; you work hard and you play hard. And I was no exception, although I know a number of people who were a lot worse than me. I was prepared for the time and cost of litigation; I wasn't prepared for the company climbing into my shorts.

—Jack, bond trader, age 31

• Finally, consider your next job. Prospective employers will not jump at the notion of hiring someone who has sued or is suing a former employer. Extinguish your hopes if you think you'll ever hear your prospective employer encouraging his colleagues with, *"Hey, let's hire this guy. He'll really keep us on our toes!"* Most prospective employers, despite your otherwise positive reputation in the business, will conclude that having once sued, you will do it twice. This is the identical standard used against dogs that bite. Even if your prospective employer is nothing like the jerks at your former company who forced you into court, they'll never know that and won't want to take the risk of finding out.

So, should you sue? Only as a last resort. Reflect that moral victories untainted by large cash settlements have always been the province of martyrs and saints, not successful businesspeople. Should you be fully apprised of your rights, and can an attorney help you during your negotiations? Absolutely. Using an attorney this way may make the difference between achieving what you wanted through negotiation, in the first place, as well as helping you avoid the rigors of the courthouse, in the second.

# PART THREE

# THE
# NEGOTIATIONS

# 7

# GETTING WHAT YOU
# WANT FROM
# NEGOTIATIONS

If you've done the math, you've probably concluded that your company's standard separation package will provide you with only the shakiest of bridges between your old job and the new one you'll find. To make up for this, you'll have to resign yourself to either working continuous shifts at the Super Burger or negotiating with your employer to enhance the standard separation package. Negotiating with your employer, even if you feel hesitant about the idea right now, is definitely the best and most productive way to go.

But what will you negotiate for?

## WHAT YOU'RE NOT
## NEGOTIATING FOR

Let's begin with what you *will not* be negotiating for: *You will not be negotiating for issues of ego.* Now is not the time to ask that your nameplate be retired and bronzed, or that your telephone be answered by someone with a cultured accent. Neither will you demand that the company order your former supervisor to recite an ode to your virtue while kneeling in his underwear. The company would probably be happy to give you these things if they thought that would satisfy you and save them from offering you a decent separation package. What you *will* be negotiating for is money, in one form or another.

The components of your separation package will vary depending on your former position in the company, your tenure, and the number of photos you have of key individuals consorting with animal friends. (This isn't a joke. The sensitive information you have about goings-on in the company—what you've been privy to, whether it's real or perceived—will improve your leverage.) Your relationship with your supervisor, your past job performance, your contributions to the company, and the underlying reasons for your termination will establish the parameters for what you can obtain. It will then be up to your preparation and negotiating skills to enhance the package.

☞ It is also imperative that you understand the value the company places on what you're bargaining for. Some of the things that are most important to you may be a matter of complete indifference to your employer. On the other hand, some things you are prepared to throw away may seem very important to your company. Since negotiations are a give-and-take process, things you're willing to concede may actually be the other's prime objective. Don't concede anything quickly.

## WHAT YOU ARE NEGOTIATING FOR

The following list of elements might be included in your enhanced separation package. Although not all of the elements discussed here possess a strict dollar denomination, all have real value:

- Severance increased
- Health and other insurance coverages extended
- Vacation, sick, and personal days paid
- Bonuses or incentives paid or prorated
- Noncash benefits extended
- Departure date changed
- Retirement benefits enhanced
- Lump-sum payments exchanged for salary continuation (or the reverse)

## Severance Increased

Only a few states have laws requiring an employer to pay terminated employees any kind of separation pay or severance. Yet, just about all large employers have policies on severance payments and they are typically outlined in a formal summary plan description. Structuring severance payments by a written policy isn't gratuitous—it's in the company's interest to establish such a policy that they can claim to be "standard" because (1) by doing so they can hold down costs, since their standard benefits will invariably be conservative, and, (2) because they can protect themselves from claims of unfairness, since everyone is offered the standard policy. Although exceptions to standard policy are made, companies are understandably concerned about creating exceptions that could be construed as precedents for the future.

☞ In order to be considered for an enhanced, non-standard separation package, you'll have to demonstrate an employment history so unique your company will feel secure such a history won't be replicated at any point in the future.

Smaller companies tend not to have policies but instead craft departure packages on an individual basis—which could either be helpful or hurtful, depending on the largesse extended to you.

A formula is generally used to calculate severance pay. The most common severance pay formula is one week's pay for each year of service, often with a cap of twenty-six or fifty-two weeks. More liberal formulas increase the multiple at five and ten years of service. Under a scaled formula, tenure really counts, and an employee would receive compensation as follows:

### Severance Policy Formula

| Years of Service | Rate of Compensation | Calculation |
| --- | --- | --- |
| 1 to 4 Years | 1 Week of pay | 2 yrs x 1 wk = 2 wks of pay |
| 5 to 9 Years | 2 Weeks of pay | 6 yrs x 2 wks = 12 wks of pay |
| 10 Years or more | 3 Weeks of pay | 11 yrs x 3 wks = 33 wks of pay |

If your company's policy is a flat formula (that is, the same number of weeks given to everyone without a multiple applied to greater years of service) and you have longer tenure, you can suggest that a formula honoring tenure should be applicable to you. If you know how many people have service at a level comparable to yours, and the number is comparatively small, let the company know. This will reassure them that the potential group of people with comparable service who can argue for the same policy exception is not threatening. If you don't know how many there are, challenge the company to tell you how many hundreds of thousands of people will fall into the same boat!

If you argue unsuccessfully for a change in formula, propose a solution outside the policy that will beneficially impact the terms of the formula. If you've had a break in service (worked for the company, left, and returned), ask that your service be "bridged." Bridged service is the sum of the time you worked for your company initially, plus your second tour of duty, with no credit for the intervening time you were gone. For example, you worked for your company for ten years, left for three years, then returned and worked for another ten years. If your service were bridged, you would be given credit for twenty years of service. As you can see from the scaled example given above, someone at nine years of service gets eighteen weeks of pay; someone with ten years gets thirty weeks— a difference of twelve weeks of pay. Every extra year of service helps, particularly if you're close to a new pay threshold.

Another argument you should consider is that your salary has been artificially depressed. You might cite a salary freeze that prevented you from realizing the compensation due you, had it not been for the freeze. If applicable, mention a supervisor who may have spoken about raising your pay but then couldn't come through for you. (The best are people who are with the company and will support your story; second best are those who have left.)

If you can make a good case for this, argue that a more encompassing compensation figure should be used when employing the standard formula. Frequently, only base salary is considered part of the severance formula. Your bonus, commissions, lump-sum payments, or stock options, which aren't part of your base pay but a substantial component of your overall compensation, are not included. Refer to memos, if any, that speak about how the company's compensation package is weighted toward longer-term incentives. Remind management that the company is responsible for cutting off your longer-term earnings potential, so you want to see that money in your severance pay today.

☞ Don't forget that rank has its privileges. Many companies structure their severance pay policies so that senior officers receive more. This is written into the summary plan description in very small type because it tends to upset those not as senior and as fortunate.

---

### Notes from the Firing Line

*If you were originally hired for a specialized task that the company now no longer needs, monitor your status. You may decide to take preemptive action:*

I was at a key point in my career and earning a fair amount of money. But when the company was taken over and new management needed to keep people like me from bolting, I was promised that if I were terminated down the road, I would receive triple my usual severance. However, before anyone had a chance to pull this new company together, we were bought by yet another company. This company asked me to stay, and I agreed. However, after a while, it became clear that my new job was all title and no responsibility. I began to suspect that the new company, learning of my triple severance deal, had offered to keep me around so that they could get rid of me at reduced severance later on. I went to my boss and told him it was crazy to keep me around at my salary, with no responsibilities to speak of—my departure could save the company a fortune. All I wanted in return was my triple severance deal. It wasn't difficult to gently remind my boss that a court would look unfavorably at an employer who made up fictitious jobs just to save on the severance package. My logic was rewarded amply. I received triple severance and found a new job quickly.

—Walt, marketing executive, age 44

Remember to read all the footnotes in your hiring agreement or the summary plan description, since you may qualify for an executive package that sets a minimum payment if your years of service fall short. Executives typically receive either the formula based on their years of service or six months to a year of severance, whichever is greater. And the cap on payments of twenty-six or fifty-two weeks sometimes doesn't apply, either. While this may seem unfair to those who don't qualify, companies often hire senior people to effect a quick fix in some area of the company or in its products. If the fix doesn't take—or if the problem is solved—the senior executive may no longer be doing anything useful. The company fully understands the implications of turning someone out on the street who has high compensation and will have a potentially difficult time in securing employment at a similar level. Equally, companies realize that senior management often serves at the pleasure of the chief executive officer. When management teams change, the terminations that ensue are somewhat "no-fault" in nature. (The adage "In with the new, out with the old" often becomes *In with my college roommate; out with your brother-in-law."*)

## Health and Other Insurance Coverages Extended

In the United States, until recently, we acknowledged the proposition that as day follows night, when you lose your job, you lose your benefits. In much of the rest of western civilization, people find this strange and perplexing. When workers in most European countries lose their jobs, their medical coverage continues. That's because the coverage is provided by the government, not by their employer. Only in the United States does the insult of the loss of benefits get added to the injury of losing your job.

Until the mid-1980s, terminated workers faced serious problems finding replacement health insurance. The first relief was a law known as COBRA (Consolidated Omnibus Budget Reconciliation Act of 1986). Under COBRA, employers of more than twenty employees are legally mandated to offer most employees who are involuntarily terminated the option of purchasing health insurance coverage that lasts for eighteen months following the date of termination. However, the coverage is costly. Your employer can charge you the combined premium—what was formerly your share and the company's—plus a 2 percent administrative fee. This means that if your premium was subsidized by your employer—you paid 25 percent of the premium and your employer paid 75 percent—your new cost will be four times what you paid before. Here's an example: When you were employed, your total premium was $100. As an employee, you paid 25 percent, or $25 per month. Your employer subsidized the rest, paying 75 percent, or $75. Now, under COBRA, you will bear not only the full cost of the total premium, $100, but also a 2 percent surcharge, bringing the grand total to $102. (That, by the way, is only a simple illustration. It's doubtful that anyone would pay a COBRA health premium of only $102.00 per month. A more realistic amount would be $700 to $900 for family coverage.)

It may be difficult to believe that your ex-employer would want to be sure you were getting a good deal in any aspect of your separation, but many are extremely sensitive to health insurance issues. This is especially true where either you or a member of your family has a known medical condition. Think of the inequity: At a time when you can least afford to pay for a substantially increased premium because you're out of work, you'll be *grateful* to obtain your costly coverage under COBRA. And up to the passage of the Health Insurance Portability and Accountability Act of 1996 (HIPAA), effective July 1, 1997, paying an increased COBRA premium was not only your best alternative, it may have been the only game in town. Prior to the 1996 Health Insurance Act, if you or a member of your family had a preexisting medical condition, a less expensive carrier wouldn't issue a policy (or it would be astronomically priced!) and your new employer could either exclude the preexisting condition from coverage or make you sit out a waiting period before issuing coverage. Under the 1996 law, you are guaranteed the right to purchase an individual policy at a rate that is no higher than the premiums charged to someone who is in good health and purchasing the same policy. And if you obtain employment elsewhere, your new employer can exclude you or a member of your family from coverage because of a preexisting condition for a period of no more than twelve months, a period that must be reduced by the length of prior continuous coverage.

Effective January 1, 1997, COBRA also provides for an extension of coverage for an additional eleven months following the first eighteen months if you or a member of your family is, in the opinion of the Social Security Administration, deemed disabled at any time during the first sixty days of continuation coverage. Since the process is a lengthy one, don't wait to check it out through Social Security to learn whether this is applicable to you.

☞ Your first choice would be to have your employer continue your benefits until you find your next job, where you'll be covered under the new employer's policy. Your second choice would be to have your health benefits continued for some period of time— a year, for instance, or the duration of your separation pay. If your employer won't pay the full cost of the premium, ask to continue to split the cost. All these accommodations give you a lower cost basis and postpone the time when you'll start to exhaust your COBRA benefits. And after you exhaust those benefits, you can buy an individual policy on an equal footing with someone who is in good health purchasing that same policy.

Companies covered by COBRA that provide dental insurance treat that coverage in a similar fashion to health insurance continuation. If yours doesn't, review chapter 12, which discusses replacing insurance.

In addition, you may qualify for a leave of absence under the Family Medical Leave Act of 1993 (FMLA), which applies to employers with fifty or more employees. An employee who has worked at least 1,250 hours during the twelve months before the leave is requested may take an unpaid leave of absence for a total of twelve weeks during any twelve-month period. Leave may be taken in situations involving the birth or adoption of a child, or the serious health condition of the employee or the employee's spouse, parent, or child. Group health benefits must be maintained during the leave. While this leave may be unpaid, it keeps you on your employer's payroll for up to twelve additional weeks before you're officially terminated. Thus it preserves your medical benefits for an additional three months before you start your COBRA benefits. Check with your human resources department and read your employee handbook, which describes how the legal requirements combine with your employer's policy on paid/unpaid leaves of absence.

Insurance benefits such as life and long-term disability are not covered under COBRA. However, the last thing a company wants to see is a headline in the newspaper that you've died from a heart attack as a result of the shock of losing your job with the company. In your company's CEO's nightmare, the picture with the story shows your family, with your absence conspicuous, lamenting the loss of your life insurance coverage because the company canceled it on the day you were terminated. To spare the company— and of course yourself—this agony, ask to continue your participation *at least* through the term of your severance payments (try for six months or a year), or best of all, until you find a new job. Also, review chapter 12, which discusses obtaining replacement insurance.

## Vacation, Sick, and Personal Days Paid

Companies often modify their policies about payout of unused vacation, sick, and personal days when dealing with laid-off employees. In general, most companies don't pay terminated employees for unused days except when that policy is overridden by state law. (States requiring companies to pay are listed in the table below.) *A layoff may prompt generosity; if it doesn't, you should*—particu-

### States Requiring Companies to Pay for Unused Vacation Days Upon Termination

| | | |
|---|---|---|
| Arizona | Louisiana | North Dakota |
| California | Maine | Ohio |
| Colorado | Maryland | Oklahoma |
| District of Columbia | Massachusetts | Oregon |
| Illinois | Minnesota | Pennsylvania |
| Indiana | Montana | Puerto Rico |
| Iowa | Nebraska | Utah |
| Kansas | New Hampshire | Wyoming |

larly if you can argue that you seldom used this type of time off because of your dedication to the company and the inhuman hours you worked. Lay it on thick.

---

### Notes from the Firing Line

*If you believe your accomplishments on the job were unique, you may be able to persuade your employer to extend additional financial recognition:*

Just before my transfer to another division, my company cited me and seven others in my group for perfect attendance. Then shortly after my transfer, the company went through a reorganization. My division was sold, and I lost my job. This seemed bitterly ironic to me at the time; after all, they'd just told me by a special award how valuable I was to them. In any event, I was able to turn that award to my advantage. When the company offered me the standard separation package, I held out for payment of unused time off. I argued that my dedication to my work had been acknowledged as extraordinary, as evidenced by the award I received. Since none of the other members of the group of eight who had also received the award had been members of the division that was sold, I thought I could give the company a valid reason for making an exception in my case. They understood that the seven other guys weren't going to show up and demand, "Me, too." I also suggested that the company be doubly safe and term the additional payment something other than "unused time off," because that made the payment unique and special (which is why these payments are often coined "special payments"), and the company agreed.

—Craig, electrical engineer, age 35

---

## Bonuses or Incentives Paid or Prorated

Bonus compensation comprises a significant portion of some people's total compensation and an insignificant portion of others. Most bonus plans have discretionary components relating to the size of the pool to be paid, the translation of the value of an individual's performance to hard bonus dollars, or the impact of the company's annual financial performance on the pool.

☞ Sometimes all the subjectivity and cloudiness surrounding who is paid what bonus and when works to your employer's benefit—it's hard to hit a moving target.

Still, as a negotiator, look at this as an opportunity to propose as many viable formulas as you can to calculate what you would have received had you been there several months down the road. An average of your past three years' bonuses? An average of what others in similar jobs received if your bonus was very large? Your weight divided by your shoe size? Devel-

---

### Notes from the Firing Line

*If you've been terminated midyear, and a full year's bonus is important to your total compensation, argue for fair treatment:*

My boss couldn't make a quick decision if his life depended on it. When my department was RIF'd—reduced in force—I was on the original layoff list. Then I was off it. Then on it. Off, again. Finally, on. By this time we were entering the summer, and I knew that no one was going to even consider hiring me until September. Try to find someone in his or her office on a Friday in August, let alone someone in a position to make me an offer. I went back to my boss's boss, who fortunately had the ability to decide something in under ten days. I told him that I had worked a half-year, I was entering the job market at the worst time of the year, and there was no way I would be given a full year's bonus from my next employer. I pointed out that it was my boss's inability to decide if I was coming or going that was the cause of the problem. I asked the company to pay my bonus on a prorated basis since they were responsible for my delayed job-hunting start. He thought about it, and then he agreed.

—Jeff, programmer, age 31

oping creative but wholly credible formulas for this and the other components of your package is key to a successful negotiation.

If you're terminated after the midpoint of the year and you don't view your bonus as a significant portion of your total compensation, use it as a bargaining chip and trade it for something else. On the other hand, if your bonus is a significant contributor to your total compensation, argue strenuously for payment based on the half-year worked. Also argue fair treatment—a new employer likely won't pay you a full year's bonus—you'll be prorated to half.

Many companies maintain the policy of paying bonuses only to employees who were on the payroll at the time the bonus was paid, even though the bonus had already been earned. If your company places you in this situation, here are two arguments to circumvent the restriction:

1. Look at past practices—generally exceptions abound and the bonuses paid contrary to policy are often termed "special payments."
2. If the bonus payment date is close, argue that you be allowed to remain on the payroll on a leave of absence, vacation, or consulting basis (paid or unpaid) in order to satisfy the letter of the policy.

Incentive payments or commissions are often paid on schedules that separate the payment date from the date earned. "Earned" dates are usually defined with reference to either the date of sale or the date of customer payment. Compensation payments to employees may coincide with the date of sale, the date of customer payment, or a draw date, which represents a calendarizing of earnings.

☞ If you have received an advance against commissions (which is an overpayment, because it's prior to the earned date) don't leap to your feet and volunteer to return the money. Your company can demand repayment, but in the meantime you're holding a valuable bargaining chip. If the earned date of your commission is after your scheduled date of departure, use the strategies outlined above for obtaining bonus payments that would usually be paid after your date of departure.

## Noncash Benefits Extended

Sometimes the hang-up in improving the separation package stems from the manner in which the company books its expenses. Provision of noncash benefits gives your company an opportunity to absorb the increased expense of your separation package in an inconspicuous manner or move it to a better line on the budget. This reduces the company's concerns about cost or exceptions to policy.

Noncash benefits are limited only by your imagination. They always make good trading fodder, because you're relinquishing something that has a limited impact on your immediate cash flow. Here are some ideas of what to ask for:

***Accelerated or preserved stock/option vesting.*** Options and stock awards are constructed as future payments for past service. They usually vest at a date or dates in the future, and all unvested options are usually forfeited at the time of termination. Your argument is that the company has reduced the life span of your job, thereby diminishing your ability to sit back and watch your options or stock vest. Your request is either to accelerate the vesting period of your unvested portion so all options or a great number of options are exercisable before you leave, or to preserve your vesting schedule despite your departure date. Frequently, people choose salary continuation if their options are especially valuable, because that enables their employers to continue their vesting schedules during the period of their salary continuation without worrying about "making exceptions." Your argument is fairness: to preserve the value of compensation for services *already* rendered, which may no longer be payable to you through no (or little) fault of your own.

Stock options are often the province of the highly paid, but increasingly companies are using them to reward employees at all levels of the corporation. Your company's annual report or a plan document may give you a clue about how the more senior players' option vesting schedules were treated when those more fortunate than you were terminated. Ask, and maybe ye shall receive.

***Retirement credits or added/bridged years of service to satisfy compensation formulas.*** As discussed in the section on severance pay, many companies are reluctant to change preset compensation formulas. Retirement plans are often governed by federal law (Employee

Retirement Income Security Act of 1974 [ERISA] and the Older Workers Benefit Protection Act of 1991), and their favorable tax treatment is governed by stringent rules. Employers are concerned that exceptions could jeopardize the plan's tax-favored status. Your request is that your employer make a change to your status, *outside of the plan*, which beneficially affects your treatment under the plan. For example, eligibility for your employer's retiree medical plan requires that you be a minimum age, say fifty-five, with a minimum number of years of service, say ten. If you satisfy the age requirement but not the service requirement (hypothetically, you have only nine years of service), your employer can grant you a phantom year of service. You could then be eligible for retiree medical insurance without creating an exception to the plan, which would happen if the benefit were to be given to someone with only nine years of service.

Or your employer can operate within the plan and, as with the stock options, accelerate your vesting schedule. If your retirement plan requires that you have ten years of service to be vested and you have only nine, ask to be given accelerated vesting for the missing year.

***Employer 401(k) and profit-sharing contributions continued.*** Many employer contributions to employee-funded savings plans are made at year's end. If you leave before the end of the year, ask to receive the contribution on a prorated basis. Or ask to be carried on your employer's benefit program during the period of your salary continuation, as though you had completed the year. Or ask that the equivalent amount of the contribution be applied to another benefit that is important to you.

***Annuities paid up.*** Similar to stock and options, annuities are often awarded for past service, and it isn't your fault that the period during which the annuity would be fully funded has been abridged. Ask to have the payments made on an accelerated basis or to preserve the original time frame for payment, even though you'll have departed.

***Relocation costs covered.*** These costs, if you've been moved by the company before termination, may be reimbursed if you combine a fairness plea with a suggestion of guilt. (*"My spouse still hasn't forgiven me for moving the family across the country. But I assured* *her this was going to be a great opportunity for us. . . ."*) In addition, if you're within striking distance of retirement, this could be an opportunity to resettle in a desirable location at minimal cost to your employer or you. Relocation expenses include house-hunting costs, temporary living costs, direct moving expenses, indirect expenses, mortgage differentials, housing subsidies, settling-in allowances, and other unusual expenses (for example, moving your yacht). These are accounted differently from other benefit expenses and may provide the company with an opportunity to dispense some quiet largesse.

***Loans forgiven or not repaid immediately.*** Company loans, even those from your own money, such as from a 401(k) or a credit union, represent nontaxable benefits. (Incidentally, your employer is not mandated by any law to pay out your 401(k) when you leave. If you have an outstanding loan, suggest that your 401(k) along with your loan remain at your company even though new funds can't be added to it. Continue to pay yourself back on the existing schedule while using the funds.) Preserve as many loans as you can, since they often represent a minimal investment for your employer and a major replacement headache for you. Better yet, loans—except those from qualified plans, such as a 401(k)—can be forgiven by your employer. It's practically an untraceable benefit to you and prompts few fears of opening the exception floodgates. Keep in mind that a loan that is forgiven becomes taxable in the year it's forgiven. As a practical matter then, set aside money to pay the taxes, or obtain a bank loan to pay the taxes. Tax considerations aside, it remains a great benefit.

***Consulting work provided.*** Consulting work affords you two benefits—income and the message it carries to future employers, which is: *My former employer valued my work, so my departure from them is no reflection on my ability to do a good job.* Many consulting practices have risen from the ashes of a termination. If you're on board as a consultant, many of the issues around your continuing membership in various benefit programs are easily resolved.

***Memberships, associations, company discounts, family benefits, and perks continued or preserved.*** A fertile imagination and a good list of *all* the benefits you've received during your employment with your company are all that you'll need here. Just to stimulate your thinking, consider the following:

---

### Notes from the Firing Line

*If you've borrowed money from your company, you should consider using the loan as leverage in your negotiations:*

I've always prided myself on being financially attuned, and I'm the ultimate pragmatist. It's no understatement to say that my boss hated me and I despised her. Anyhow, I knew she was looking for a clean shot at me. You know what they say: If you look long and hard enough, it will happen. My relationship with a key vendor had never been good, and finally (or so my boss claimed) she had to choose between them and me. Two guesses who she chose. As I mentioned, I'm pretty good at this stuff, so in preparation for her little announcement, I went to the employee credit union and the benefits department and took out as many loans as I could. So in addition to my severance money, I had two loans that were sitting in a bond fund earning interest for me. I'd never stiff the company for the money, but it did provide some extra issues for discussion as I was heading for the door.

—Jim, display manager, age 39

---

Health club membership
Annual physical exam
Children's scholarships
Legal consultation services
Country or lunch club memberships
Tax preparation services
Company car and parking
Elder or child care services
Employee discounts on company services or products
Telephones, voice mail, computers
Paid attendance at trade shows or educational seminars
Matching of educational or charitable gifts
Tuition reimbursement

Even if you can't get payment for these, they make great trading items.

***Outplacement services as well as office and secretarial support provided or increased.*** Although we strongly recommend that you hold on to your office for as long as you can (if you're out of sight, you're out of mind—and you want to remain on a number of people's minds until you close your deal), outplacement, office, and secretarial support services are helpful in minimizing the costs associated with finding a new job or starting your own business. This includes typing, voice mail or phone answering services, printing of resumes and cover letters, long distance telephone access, and even reimbursement of travel expenses associated with your job search.

***Good and "restricted" references predetermined.*** Knowing what the company will say about you and restricting who can speak on behalf of the company can be essential in helping you get a new job. It's also essential in preserving your peace of mind. Society's attitude toward people who've lost their jobs has turned around lately, thanks to volcanic and scandalous corporate reorganizations that displaced many thousands of qualified employees. The old, unvoiced assumption that concludes, *"Hey! He's been let go? Must be totally incompetent, or a crook!"* is probably no longer *automatically* made. Even so, you may need to allay the fears of prospective employers about your employability. Here's the dilemma: Most companies have narrow reference policies. *"Sorry. We only provide dates of service and job titles"* is about all the information they'll release, officially. Your company doesn't want to meet you again in a defamation lawsuit. The unofficial reality is markedly different, however. Even a moderately skilled reference checker can get plenty of information from a former employer. If someone's out to do you harm, the unofficial "information" leaks can be stupendous, truly damaging, and virtually untraceable. Unstopped, these malicious leaks occur even if you're leaving the company through no fault of your own. The leaks occur because (1) people who leave the company may be considered traitors by those still employed, and/or (2) everyone loves to spread gossip.

As part of your negotiations, review what will be said about you. This act is constructive because it puts your company on notice that you understand the little reference game and how it's played. Suggest how you would like your references to be handled, and get agreement about who will be the official spokesperson for the company. Gently remind your employer that while you remember that the company's official policy is to say nothing substantive, you know how these things go.

Several states have service letter laws that require an employer to provide a written explanation of your work history and the reasons for your departure. If you lived or worked in Kansas, Maine, Minnesota, Missouri, Montana, Nevada, Texas, or Washington, getting a copy of a service letter can't hurt your reference cause and it may help. Typically, you must make the request for the letter in writing within five days of your termination date.

A note of reality here: The more senior you are, the more useless a letter of reference. If your new employer wants one, consider whether they're playing with the 1990s version of a full deck. And don't make important concessions during your negotiations to get a letter of reference.

## Departure Date Changed

Changing the timing of your departure from the company may be to your advantage in certain circumstances. If you feel that leaving your job *before* your termination would solve some problems, or if you feel that *extending* your employment beyond the cutoff date your employer wants to impose will help, don't hesitate to propose it. Here are the pros and cons for both strategies:

*Leave early.* This one takes nerve: You preempt the termination discussion by going to your boss and discussing the telltale signs that something is happening to your position. By offering to leave early, before you're officially fired, you save the company all the money that they would otherwise pay for your salary, benefits, real estate and communications costs, travel and other expenses, and staff members tied directly to you, such as secretaries or personal assistants. Calculate a number that you think is reflective of those expenses and ask for a fair division of the savings between you and the company.

☞ You should keep in mind, in order to leave early, you'll need to expedite the cleanup of your responsibilities. And while it may be appropriate for you to bail out early, your sense of honor should prompt you to consider your staff. If they're talented, make an effort to place them elsewhere so that they don't get swept out the door in your wake.

*Leave later.*   Instead of leaving early, your circumstances might prompt you to leave later. If you're part of a reduction in force, demonstrate that your work is essential and can't be successfully concluded when everyone else goes. Ask for a "stay put" bonus to persuade you to remain at a job without any future prospects. Better yet, term the payment you'll receive something other than severance—call it "consulting pay." This will proclaim your excellent relationship with your former employer to future employers.

## Retirement Benefits Enhanced

As mentioned earlier, many companies have formulas that combine age and tenure to determine eligibility for early retirement. If you're close to retirement but it's no cigar, ask to have the missing element granted in recognition of your long-term contributions to the company. If you're close to a threshold for vesting and you won't make the cutoff date because of the layoff, point out that you'd be happy to continue working—the company's decision to terminate you prevents you from accruing what you worked long and hard to achieve. This argument is particularly suited to unvested employer-matching contributions to employee saving plans and retiree medical coverage.

## Lump-Sum Payments Exchanged for Salary Continuation (or the Reverse)

It may be a matter of complete indifference to your employer, but you should carefully consider whether you want your separation pay in a lump sum or carried over a number of months (or years, if you're so fortunate) as salary continuation. The benefit of receiving a lump sum is that you'll have all your money at once; it's yours to do with as you wish, and the question of having your payments stopped when you take a new job is avoided.

The benefit of salary continuation is that your employer can more easily continue you in benefits and other programs, since the process is similar to regular employment with a periodic paycheck. In addition, by spreading the payments over a longer period of time, you may moderate the tax bite. Payments received in a year when your income is lower will consequently be taxed at a lower rate—which may be the *second* year of unemployment if you're laid off in the latter part of the *first* calendar year.

The downside of receiving a lump sum is deciding what to do with it. Review chapter 13 for some specific investment advice. Receiving a lump sum also takes you out of most benefit programs immediately, since you are no longer "on the payroll."

The downside of salary continuation is that some employers require forfeiture of remaining separation pay when new employment is secured. This is easier to enforce when your payments are made on a continuing basis. Also, if your employer's financial solvency is questionable, continuing payments puts your money at risk. We strongly recommend that these considerations be reviewed by your financial adviser.

While the company may not be in a position to grant you all that you've asked for, your emphasis should always be on making requests that are reasonable under the circumstances. If you're aware that others have received exceptional treatment in the past, now is the time to allude to that, as well. Because you've presented your counteroffer and entered fully into subsequent discussions, with their natural give and take, the moment of termination has been changed irrevocably in your emotional and, we hope, financial favor.

Finally, if your formal attempts at securing an enhanced separation package are not going as well as you'd like, there remains the *informal* route to enhancement, also known as nagging. It may be a cliché, but the squeaky wheel quite often gets the grease.

---

### Notes from the Firing Line

*If nothing else works for you, try whining:*

I can't make up my mind about Fred: He must have been one of the most obnoxious people ever born. Even when things were going well for him, he always had a complaint. When he was downsized as part of a big layoff, he was assigned to me for outplacement counseling. He'd come to my office every day, and in that truly annoying way he had, he would beg me for something else. "What about my unpaid vacation time?" he'd whine. "What about my laptop? Can I take that?" "Can you update my parking permit for me?" I'm ashamed to say that in the end I agreed to every one of his complaints and demands. Anything to get that man out of my office and out of my life! Even so, I can't make up my mind about him: He was either the luckiest loser I've ever come across, or (and I sometimes suspect this) the shrewdest negotiator.

—Linda, human resources, age 28

# 8

# THE INNER GAME OF
# NEGOTIATIONS

*Strategy. Negotiations.* Perhaps not the uppermost thoughts on your mind at this moment. What you're probably feeling are grief and anger. Accepting the loss of a job you've poured your heart into is as difficult as accepting the death of a close friend. At first you deny it happened at all; then after you accept it as reality, you grow angry. Feeling really angry now is natural, but be careful. While it's tempting to indulge yourself, don't waste time fantasizing about splattering your supervisor over the walls and carpet with an assault weapon. It does not serve your goals to wave your good-byes while exiting via the window. (Just think how terrible they'll feel when they see you in your grave!) All these plans come under the category of *revenge*. It might feel good to get it out of your system, but contrary to the old saying, revenge is *not* sweet. In the long run it's self-destructive and bitter. *Revenge always ends with an epitaph dismissing you as a "disgruntled former employee."* Your objective now is to act calmly, even if you feel anything but calm.

By getting your employer to agree to a second meeting before signing yourself out of the company, you've done two positive things. First, you've opened the way for negotiation. By not signing on the dotted line, you change the nature of your relationship from one in which your employer holds all the power to one in which you share power. This shift alone may give you the ability to improve on your termination package. Second, you've bought yourself some time to develop a negotiating strategy. As we've mentioned before, a separation pay negotiation in which the employee attempts to stand on equal footing with the person terminating him or her is not desirable from the company's perspective. Therefore, it's crucial that you concentrate on how you'll handle the negotiation and get what you want from it.

# WHAT IF I'M NOT A NEGOTIATOR?

Some people, confronted by the necessity to negotiate, draw a blank. These people believe that either you're born a negotiator or you're not—and they weren't endowed with those genes at birth. But this is a false assumption. All lasting and productive human relationships involve negotiations of one sort or another. This is the case among friends, family, neighbors, co-workers, and so on. To be successful, each party must be willing to offer to the relationship what it needs and also be prepared to ask for what he or she needs from it. Successful and satisfying negotiations produce win-win situations—achievable even by someone with little experience. (See chapter 9 for a step-by-step short course in the basics of negotiating.)

## Developing Your Negotiating Strategy

Negotiating your separation package will not require you to be a master of the battlefield, like Patton or Powell; an accomplished manipulator of people, like Machiavelli; or a chess champion like Fischer. If you've ever won at checkers or even tic-tac-toe, you already have an intuitive understanding of strategy development. That is, you need to create a framework for your negotiation and what you want to get out of it. And don't hesitate to think hard about these things because you fear that attempting to change the separation package you've been offered will result in the withdrawal of the offer altogether. Almost invariably, company policy or legal considerations require that they not retract their offer.

Keep in mind that the separation package offered by your employer is negotiable. It's neither final nor complete until you accept it. If you try to improve it, the worst that can happen is you won't get what you want. Since you've already been terminated, you've got nothing further to lose by trying.

---

### Notes from the Firing Line

*You may be new at negotiating, but if you're calm and reasonable—no matter what others at the negotiating table are—you'll have a better chance of getting the separation package you need:*

In all my years practicing law, I can't remember a dumber encounter than the one between my client, an employer, and an employee he wanted to fire. My client was emotional; he really hated his employee and was just itching to can him—pick a reason, any reason. When the employee asked for some very reasonable concessions, my client used the occasion to go off the deep end. Before I could stop him, he had screamed that the employee would get nothing, the employee was nothing, and nobody would ever hire him again. Well, that proved wrong: The employee sued and recovered a large judgment, then he went on to find a terrific job elsewhere. Come to think of it, to call my client's temper tantrum 'stupid' is kind. It was really idiotic."

—Rob, managing partner of law firm, age 52

---

Unless you have compelling evidence that your firing was unlawful (see chapter 5), or you know where the company bodies are buried and you're determined to try blackmail, you will depend a great deal on the goodwill you've generated by your years of service and the closeness of your personal relationships within the company or key relationships outside the organization to help your negotiations. *Bringing external pressure to bear on the negotiations puts you on a more equal footing with your employer.*

A successful separation negotiating strategy consists of five parts. To put your strategy into action, you will now proceed to:

1. Assemble your allies and marshal support.
2. Use all persuasion at your command.
3. Present your counteroffers and try to find common ground.
4. If negotiations reach a stalemate, remind your employer that "fault" is a two-way street.
5. Threaten legal action only after you're given up all hope that your negotiation can remain amicable.

## ALLIES AND SUPPORT

Most businesses rely on hierarchical structures or chains of command. Your supervisor reports to his or her supervisor, who in turn reports to another, and so on up the line. In such settings the idea of going above your own boss for support and leverage may seem suicidal. If you were still employed, it probably would be. But you've been terminated. You're already dead, and they can't kill you twice. As with your original decision to negotiate your separation package because you had nothing to lose by it, so you'll lose nothing by going up, under, around, and through your company's hierarchy, tapping the good offices of friends and supporters.

☞ Do not limit your contact at your company to the person who terminated you. While it might seem logical and ethical to do this, you would be making a tactical error.

At the same time, you would lose an opportunity to raise the negotiating process to a whole new level. The person who gave you the bad news may have been your supervisor or someone from human resources. As we discussed in chapter 3, his or her job was limited to (a) telling you that you've been terminated and making sure you got through the emotional stage of denial, and (b) persuading you to sign a release that acknowledged your termination, accepted the company's separation offer, extinguished your right to sue, and got you out of their hair as rapidly as possible. By bringing others into the negotiation, you announce that you are not a cast-out sinner afraid to show your face among worthy company citizens. You are in fact walking with your head up and straightforwardly reminding others that "There but for the grace of God" go they. In the limited time you have until your negotiation meeting (often a period of just twenty-four or seventy-two hours), plan a campaign to rally support.

### Who Should You Call On?

Your critical allies include:

• *Managers and executives senior to the person who terminated you.* Choose those with whom you've had a good relationship at work and, if possible, a good relationship out of the office.

- *People who are familiar with your work and think well of you.* These could include clients and customers with whom you've worked closely, important vendors, and people who are responsible for revenue.
- *Your mentor.* Perhaps this is someone who recruited you to the organization or groomed you along the way. Ideally, it's someone important and well regarded in your company.
- *Human resources people.* These people have been trained to respect policy and past practice. Although they work for the company, they'll be helpful to you if you've discovered that others have received separation benefits in excess of stated policy. Look for people regarded as fair and independent thinkers.

## What Should You Ask For?

This will depend on your needs and those of your family, and on your particular relationship with your allies. As discussed in chapter 7, an enhanced separation package contains a number of components ranging from an increase in severance to an extension of cash and noncash benefits. First, assess your needs as described in chapter 4. If you have a personal relationship *and* a business relationship with some of your allies—they've been to your home and met your family—let them know about your family's specific financial problems. For example, if any of your family members requires special or ongoing medical attention, ask your allies help in getting your medical benefits extended beyond the period covered by the company's separation package. If you have children in college, ask your allies to use their influence to increase the cash or endowment portion of the separation package.

Specifics of what you request from your allies will depend on your personal situation. Whatever you do, don't whine, don't threaten, and don't pander. Instead, be sincere and realistic. Make them want to support you.

Support from important and vocal portions of the organization is compelling at times like this. Your allies elsewhere in the company are key since your fate may no longer rest exclusively in your boss's hands (his or her job could be in equal jeopardy). Because every company's culture differs, how your allies render support will differ. Sometimes all they need to do is speak with someone up the

---

### Notes from the Firing Line

*If you've made friends with influential people—whether employed by the company or having some connection outside the company—don't hesitate to call on them:*

My boss, or I should say, my ex-boss, Elliot, was a great guy. We all enjoyed working for him. After he was recruited away from the company by the competition, our department was "rightsized." I work in one of those areas where you don't see a return on your money within eight minutes, so we're always vulnerable. We all knew that in Elliot's absence we were just sitting ducks for the guys in finance to shoot at. When I was eventually laid off, my severance was pitiful because my big earnings had always come from performance bonuses. The only thing I could think to do was call Elliot. He was great about it. He called his former boss. God knows what he said, but my severance was recalculated taking into consideration my actual income from performance bonuses, not just my base pay. I'm pleased to have this chance to tell this story because for once everything worked out the way it should in a fair world.

—Don, R&D, age 40

---

line and ask that you be given consideration for an enhanced separation package. In other companies, that communication may need to be oblique. Your supporter may simply express good feelings about you and mention your many contributions to the organization in the past.

## How to Ask for Help

Asking people for their help is basically as straightforward and sincere as closing a sale—you explain what your need is, you tell them how they can help, and then you ask them for it. In order to be successful at this, you'll need to be evenhanded. Whatever you do, do not trash the company.

Say, for example, you've decided to call an influential client for help. Begin with a nonacrimonious statement of the facts, such as: *"John, I've just been told that my job is being eliminated. Of course, I wish that weren't the case, but I understand the company's need to contain costs and I'll have to respect their reasoning."*

Follow this with your request for help. You could frame this in several ways, depending on your relationship with the client. Here are three likely ways to approach the problem:

1. *Make a flattering but factual request.* "Since you are one of the company's most important accounts, I'd appreciate it if you could put in a good word on my behalf."
2. *Make a request recalling a favor that's owed you.* "You've told me on a number of occasions that I've been really helpful to you in suggesting new ways of marketing your widgets. I'd appreciate it if you could remind the company of the degree to which I've been effective on your behalf."
3. *Make a request with a promise to return the favor.* "If you could call my boss and let her know that a good separation package is what I'm aiming for, I'd appreciate it."

☞ If you have a warmer association with the person whose help you're seeking, be more specific about the help you need or why you need it. It's appropriate here to draw on the emotions for support.

Once you've identified people who can put in a good word on your behalf, apprise them of your timetable. A telephone campaign on your behalf, not asking that you retain your job but that your separation package be improved, can make all the difference. Now is not the time to keep the news of the Scarlet F (for "Fired") on your chest a secret; actively solicit people to protest on your behalf and ask that you be treated fairly. Cash in all your markers and call in all your past favors.

Finally, human resources people, having been trained to respect policy and past practice, should also be on your list of telephone calls or visits. Since you've done your job of finding out about others who have received separation packages that exceed policy (see chapter 2), remind your friends in human resources that you've been offered less than others and ask them to behave fairly. Many human resources

## Notes from the Firing Line

*You may find that your termination is a result of a supervisor's opportunistic ploy to bury you because you know too much. Rather than fight the company in court, you can use your friends to help you get an enhanced separation package:*

Cutting a deal for a good severance package that has been helped along by strong players in the company is always the best way to go. A couple of years ago during a merger, Dave, one of our most reliable salespeople with numerous supporters, was slated to be downsized. I heard about it when one of Dave's friends, a female executive, came to me. She claimed that Dave's supervisor, John, had included Dave in the downsizing because it was a convenient opportunity to get rid of somebody who could make trouble for him in the future. It seems that everyone confided in Dave, good guy that he was. And this included several women who had been sexually harassed by John—and John knew they'd gone to Dave. According to this female executive, Dave's friends in the company, who also knew what was going on, were ready to support Dave in a discrimination suit, should he decide to file. As it turned out, Dave opted to enlist his friends in a campaign to get him a better separation package. While I thought Dave had a potentially strong suit against the company that could have resulted in a significant judgment, Dave decided instead to get on with his life. He used the enhanced severance to pay for his children's college tuition.

—Arthur, labor lawyer for a national manufacturer, age 55

people will think that your references to past practices and comparable treatment of others have legal implications; they'll raise their concerns to others. This, too, will be helpful.

The value of supporters for your cause at this juncture should not be underestimated. In this situation, nice guys who focus on the goal finish first.

# PERSUASION

Your ability to get what you want will partially depend on the kindness of strangers and friends, but it will also depend on your ability to persuade them to help. You are going to invite a number of people to become involved in your plight. However, there may be reasons why some people can't or won't give you the help you need. In a worst-case scenario, if you've had difficult relations with fellow workers over the years, don't expect them to come running. One senior marketing executive with a mean temper and a tendency to bully fellow workers lost both his temper and his job one morning. Word about it spread quickly. People who had nervously returned his calls in the past now gleefully postponed responding to his anxious messages.

If your company relationships have been average or good, however, you still may not immediately receive the help you desire. In some organizations a terminated individual is looked on as an enemy, and it's dangerous for your friends to be seen consorting with you. Don't make it more dangerous than it need be for them. If you're too vocal about how the company wronged you, you'll endanger your supporters and the support they might be able to give you. Other companies may frown on people involving themselves in matters outside of their sphere of business—it's inappropriate. Be discrete when the culture demands it, but still ask for support.

If you have personal relationships, use the social contact to generate support. Remind people of your child's tuition, your spouse's illness, your dog's Purina dependency. The reasons you cite for deserving special consideration are not as important as your supporters' empathy with you and your problem. If they like you, they'll try to help you.

If your relationship with your supporters is purely professional, point to your years of service or important contributions to the business. Suggest that what has happened to you may befall others— even your allies may face termination in today's business climate. Give as many reasons as you can assemble about why in this business environment, you will need additional assistance to find a job. Point to your industry, your geography, your profession. Even point to your age—*subtly*. Remind everyone that with your years of experience, you are employable. You'll only need the support that additional compensation provides to overcome the hurdles of a protracted job search. In our economy people don't send out resumes and land jobs overnight. Your supporters should be able to relate to that.

☞ While seeking support, do not wallow in self-pity. And especially do not wallow in self-pity in the negotiation meeting. This always backfires.

If you plead poverty too loudly, for example, some employers will seize the opportunity to make a low-ball separation offer. Instead of stirring pity, the emotion you engender will be contempt, and you'll appear unable to withstand the rigors of negotiating an enhanced package. Ask for fair treatment by the company, not a handout. If you're whining, you're not winning.

Overall, when approaching your former colleagues for support, be as businesslike as possible. This is a difficult time for you, but it is also a difficult time for them, since you're asking that they put themselves on the line for you. Your calm, thoughtful, and focused attitude will signal that you've got your own situation under control. You want them to be assured that the help they'll offer will not explode in their faces through your loss of control during negotiations.

## COUNTEROFFERS AND COMMON GROUND

With the influence of your allies now affecting the person who terminated you, you'll present the counteroffer for your separation package. Return to your boss's office at the appointed hour. Be pleasant, but get down to business quickly. Explain that you've thought over the separation offer they made you and you're pleased with some of the elements, but want to talk through some of the other aspects. You'll be asked to proceed, so begin with an important issue, but not your *most* important issue. Use this opener to model the conversation you want to have. If you open with something trivial, your requests may be dismissed as trivial. If you open with the deal-breaker and don't get it because your employer doesn't recognize the seriousness of your purpose, you'll be demoralized. Give yourself a warm-up round.

Follow a pattern in which you introduce a midlevel issue, followed by something more trivial *or* something very important. (Vary the pattern so it's not obvious!) You will then have a conversation going that permits the person negotiating with you to deal with some easy issues along with thorny ones. This will build up a momentum of give-and-take, as opposed to one in which demands escalate. If you get some "No ways" along the way, you can shrug them off. Proceed to the next item on your list.

☞ To be on the safe side, your demand list should be written informally, even as cryptic notes, because the last thing you want is for someone—who may already be nervous about what you're going to ask for—to read the list over your shoulder, grow increasing alarmed, and close out the discussion with a series of unyielding "Nos." Later on, if your company wants to know how to word something in the separation agreement, you can contribute to that effort in writing. For now, keep paper out of it.

☞ Be prepared to explain and substantiate your requests so it's clear you're making an honest attempt to reach a fair agreement. Include all the improvements to your package that you *need*, along with those that you *want*. As negotiations progress, you will give up some of the things that you *want*, while seeking to retain all those that you *need*. Making concessions to your partner is what the process is all about.

By the time of your negotiation meeting, you will already have given as many reasons to your allies as you could think up for them to intervene on your behalf. Some of those were business focused; others were emotional or personal. During the negotiations with your boss or the representative from human resources, continue to be businesslike and calm. Making an emotional appeal to your allies is appropriate in your confidential talks with them, but it is not appropriate at the negotiation meeting. Such an appeal now will be unnecessary at best, and at worst will negatively distort the tone of the negotiations. Since your allies have already informed your boss or the human resources person of your personal situation, your businesslike, unemotional approach will be a relief and a token of the seriousness of your purpose.

Negotiations run a standard course. Your company has presented each element of its offer to you. Either you'll accept the element or you'll ask for something in its place or in addition. This give-and-take may go on for several meetings.

☞ Each time you meet, summarize where you stand, noting areas of agreement and disagreement.

The goal is to produce the best agreement and not the neatest penmanship, so it's always better to be looking at the person with whom you're negotiating than down at the pad on your lap. Just as extensive note-taking would have been inappropriate during your termination meeting, it's the wrong move now as well. During your discussions, you should make only brief notes. This will also help keep the atmosphere free of tension. Note-taking is intimidating, and you don't want to force the other party into studied and safe explanations of policy. That won't help your cause, which could profit by a freer give-and-take. Your lengthier notes—made after the meeting—should include compromises forged, alternatives proposed, and the status of open issues.

Negotiating is always draining. You're thinking hard, listening closely, and arguing persuasively. *When you feel you've achieved all you can in a given session, stop.* Set a new meeting date, and return, having taken the time to clear your thoughts.

When you reach a critical point of thorny contention with the person with whom you're negotiating, go back to your most influential ally and seek his or her counsel about how to resolve the sticking point in a manner that makes sense for all concerned. The act of asking for advice will again trigger the intervention that you are seeking. This doesn't mean confiding to the world how your discussions are progressing. The very opposite: Keep your counsel to yourself and discuss only the things you want to make public.

☞ One important note about your behavior: Don't humiliate or embarrass the person with whom you're negotiating by being smug about the outside intervention you've been able to bring to your discussions. Your objective is to help your negotiator feel like a partner in the resolution of the situation, not to make him or her feel one-upped. Otherwise, your negotiator may just dig in and refuse any further requests. Whenever you speak to your allies about the person with whom you're negotiating, do so with respect.

## "FAULT"—A TWO-WAY STREET

If negotiations bog down or your boss refuses to agree to your reasonable requests, you may need to escalate the discussion. This is when you'll raise the issue of "fault." At first glance the idea of bringing fault into your negotiating strategy might sound crazy. After all, unless you have been part of a mass layoff, your termination resulted from someone in power concluding that you had failed at your work. However, the blame for failure is always a two-way street.

If you've been terminated as a result of external factors—a merger, a product failure, business redundancy—the blame for causing the termination rests with those things. You aren't the cause. Thus, you can negotiate for enhanced separation pay without pointing the finger of shame directly at your boss or at you. You should argue that since the fault is bigger than either of you, it would be unfair for you alone to bear the burden of blame for the organization's failure.

Otherwise, when you're terminated, your boss will seek to lay the blame on you. Since the grounds for being terminated can have considerable range (anywhere from gross misconduct, such as theft or insubordination, to more run-of-the-mill assessments of poor job performance), the degree of fault will vary as well.

☞ The rule is: *The lesser your offense, the greater your ability to negotiate.* If your boss becomes intractable in the separation discussions, you should remind your allies that either your fault is small (which gives you greater negotiating room) or that the fault is equal and should be shared.

It should go without saying that your job performance could have been improved. *Everyone's* job performance has room for improvement. Employers make mistakes in the way they manage people, thus their job performances also have room for improvement. Your strategy will be: *Don't defend your past job performance; negotiate for your future.* Capitalize on the company's vulnerabilities to counter assertions that your job performance was a sea of mistakes.

To establish *shared* failure with your employer, suggest to your allies and to human resources any of the following that are appropriate to your situation:

- You were incorrectly selected at the outset to perform a responsibility for which you were clearly unsuited. Perhaps you left a company where you had greater tenure than you have now. You would've received more severance had you remained with that company. Or you might not have been terminated at all. (Most of this is nonverifiable, which you may consider an advantage.)
- You were improperly trained, or you weren't given the necessary resources to perform your responsibilities.

---

### Notes from the Firing Line

*Your ability to articulate your grievance will help establish that you've done your homework and you know what you're talking about:*

I'd worked for ten years for one company when a competing company offered me a terrific job with promises of job security and unparalleled opportunity. I couldn't refuse. Then six months later, I was terminated. I couldn't do anything about being fired, but in my severance negotiations I reminded them that I would have been entitled to thirty weeks of severance pay from my previous employer, had I not been induced to join them. Then I reminded them about each and every promise they made to me to get me to leave my former employer. While I never used the words "fraud," "bad faith," or "implied contract," it was really clear that I had been prepared by an attorney for the discussion. As a result, they gave me an enhanced separation package. It never hurts to ask.

—Scott, medical director, age 38

- You weren't well supervised or coached to accomplish the tasks given to you.
- You were not given sufficient and clear warning of the consequences if you failed to perform in an acceptable manner. Or no warning was given to you at all. (This may contravene the process set out in your employee handbook—check it out carefully. It's an issue that will drive the human resources people crazy and produce great support for your cause.)
- Other people were equally inept and not terminated, or were given better direction along the way, or were treated better at the time of termination.

Spending time trying, even successfully, to justify your past job performance will only bring you the standard separation package. But gently shifting the burden of guilt by pointing to management slipups stops the discussion of fault and turns it back to money—your real interest. After raising the issues outlined above, agree to move on to more pleasant topics—your separation package. You can say, *"Let's agree to disagree about the past and who was responsible for what happened. After all, even if I made mistakes, so did the company. Let's focus on reaching an agreement that will be good for all of us."*

Sharing the blame for a job done badly is an aggressive step in your effort for an improved separation package. It shifts the focus from your misdeeds to someone else's ineptitude—namely, your management's. Since neither side to the negotiations can claim perfection (especially after you've pointed out their faults so carefully), the logical step on the part of the company is to focus on what will make you quietly accept its flaws. This can only be an increase in your separation pay.

## THE THREAT OF LEGAL ACTION

Sometimes negotiations just hit a wall. Despite your best efforts to reach a compromise, someone becomes intractable or some situation just can't be dealt with satisfactorily. At this point, if you believe you have clear evidence and a good case, you should bring your attorney into the discussions with your company.

All parties to the negotiation understand that there's always legal recourse. It's the reason your employer urged you to sign away your rights at the termination meeting, and it's also the reason you've never relinquished that leverage.

☞ Warning: Once you announce your attorney's involvement, your relationship with your employer is changed forever.

It's likely the person with whom you've been negotiating will be joined shortly by either a senior human resources person or an attorney. Your separation agreement, if not reached quickly at this juncture, will never be reached in the absence of your initiating litigation. Having announced your intentions, there's no turning back.

---

### Notes from the Firing Line

*Threatening a lawsuit is serious and changes everything in a negotiation. If you're going to do it, be sure you've got the facts to back the threat:*

They tried to get rid of me by eliminating my outside sales job. Then they gave my duties to a younger man who could be paid a lower commission. I was able to stop them right there. I promised to bring a combined unjust dismissal/age discrimination case against them. Happily for me, they took my threat seriously. My boss, who had initiated the termination, was asked to step aside in the negotiations, and a settlement that made sense for all parties was achieved.

—Mike, sales, age 55

---

Having stated that you believe you have been treated unlawfully, be clear that there is evidence to support your assertions. Having said that, you may trigger an internal investigation of the events. Don't permit, even for one second, the investigation to further harass or demoralize you—this may constitute retaliation on the part of your employer, which is an impermissible form of discrimination.

Insist that the investigation and separation negotiations be concluded on an expedited basis. The ideal is to have the matter resolved to your satisfaction within two months. Longer negotiations will only result in everyone at the company losing interest in resolving the matter without litigation. You don't want to be regarded as just one more case in the company's litigation docket.

Threatening litigation is a last resort—not an opening gambit. Your objective remains to negotiate a fair deal, not to scare or intimidate your employer or be written off as all talk and no action. The best negotiations are conducted among people who respect one another. You may still believe that your employer has the upper hand. If that's the case, think of any competitive sport. Most of us rise to the occasion when playing against a better player. Our game spirals up to match our stronger competitor. While we may not win all the points, we play better and harder. That, in turn, engenders the respect of our competitor. If you are focused and professional, you're likely to prompt a similar response from your employer. The result is something everyone desires—the quiet departure. You get what you need, and it's so much more dignified than living a life of noisy desperation. You feel in control, knowing that you've covered all the bases.

# 9

# A NEGOTIATING PRIMER

If the thought of entering into negotiations makes you want to rush screaming from the building, read through this brief section on negotiation basics. As in every other situation, the security achieved through knowledge will triumph over the terror brought by ignorance. We promise.

The first thing to examine is your attitude toward negotiation and negotiators. People who don't consider themselves born negotiators are usually turned off by the image they have of the successful negotiator as either tricky, devious, and conniving or loudmouthed, inflexible, and bullying. When self-styled nonnegotiators are backed into a corner and forced to bargain, they may feel they have no choice but to adopt one of these unsavory postures. Choosing either is a mistake. Both negotiating styles may prevail in the short term, but almost always lose in the long run. The slick, sneaky operator who pulls one fast move after another often lives to see the scams backfire (as our political history so abundantly demonstrates). The bully with an inflexible attitude and intimidating manner, who browbeats opponents into an emotional or financial pulp, sooner or later loses whatever has been gained under the tide of bad will that he or she has generated. Negotiations are diminished by greed and stupidity. After all, while negotiating your separation is primarily about money, it's also about your emotional survival and dignity of life. Behaving well often results in people responding in kind.

☞ Remember: To negotiate successfully means to be prepared to give and to take, to be focused and determined, but flexible. The best negotiating outcomes result when partners to the negotiation respect each other and each tries to forge a win-win compromise.

135

## Notes from the Firing Line

*When one or another partner to a negotiation operates out of distrust, ignorance, or stupidity, a positive outcome will take a long time to achieve:*

The warehouses I managed were almost always unionized, but I had never been part of the collective bargaining process until I was promoted to assistant manager. After lengthy preparation, George, an experienced negotiator, and I walked into the conference room with these huge binders under our arms. I'll never forget how everyone just gaped. We thought we were prepared for anything. What we hadn't prepared for was the business agent sent in by the national union to help out with the local negotiations.

Right from the start, he was hostile and suspicious. He was always looking for dirty tricks or underhanded moves. It didn't matter to him what our motives were, because he was sure that we were trying to con him in some way. The negotiations took twice as long as they should have; every time we proposed a change in the contract, we were forced to wait until he had figured out that we hadn't pulled the wool over his eyes. Let me tell you, it was painful. George was far more patient with him than I could ever have been.

Finally we reached an agreement that everyone could live with, signed it, and shook hands all around. George and I went out for some well-deserved beers. I commented that he had really earned his salary dealing with this stupid union business agent. George told me something then that I've never forgotten: It's harder to reach a fair agreement with people who can't trust their own judgment and won't trust yours. He told me that it's always better to have a strong, tough, confident competitor as your negotiating partner—a worthy adversary—because that sort of negotiator brings out the best in you. And this produces the best deals.

—Leo, warehouse manager, age 44

# SMART NEGOTIATING

Your object in negotiating is naturally to *win* something, correct? But what constitutes *winning*? Well, you might reason, if someone wins, someone else loses. Wars are fought to defeat the enemy, which usually means that both sides shoot, bomb, maim, and kill enemy soldiers until one side admits defeat and begs the other for the love of God, to please stop. Is this what negotiating is about? Must a winning negotiator be ruthless and bloodthirsty? Must you debase, humiliate, and finally destroy your opponent in order to win? No, no, and no. And perhaps *winning* is not the most accurate word to describe the positive outcome of a negotiation.

☞ To get a better handle on this, mentally erase the phrase *negotiating opponent* and substitute *negotiating partner*. In a negotiation that works, both parties try to come to a resolution each can live with, more or less happily. Negotiating is not so much about vengeance as it is about accommodation. Both parties want to come away with something, and a smart negotiator will recognize this. When thinking about negotiating, it's best to decommission the war metaphors.

If you're going to be a smart negotiator, you'll have to answer some fundamental questions in preparation for your negotiating sessions:

*About yourself:*
- What do you want from the negotiation?
- Are your requests reasonable and doable?
- What do you have to do to get what you want?

*About your negotiating partner:*
- What does your negotiating partner know about the situation that you don't?
- What does your negotiating partner want from the negotiations?
- How do you and your partner differ as people? How are you the same?

*About your negotiations:*
- How will you know the best way to make the right moves at the right time?

## What Do You Want from the Negotiation?

Your answer to this question will determine whether you win or lose at the outset. An efficient way to approach the answer would be for you to write down exactly what you want, in one sentence only. Be as specific as possible. A vague answer, or one that is too general (such as, *"I want them to give me carloads of money"*) will blur your negotiations and taint the result.

Instead, examine your needs. The two areas in which you want agreement are behavioral and financial. You want your former employer to behave in a certain way toward you, and/or refrain from acting in a certain way; you want to gain the best possible financial package. Work through chapter 4 to get an accurate picture of your financial needs. Read through chapters 5, 7, and 8 to get an accurate picture of the behavioral side.

## Are Your Requests Reasonable and Doable?

Once you've analyzed your financial and behavioral needs, you must find out which of them your employer is prepared to meet or is even capable of satisfying. If you don't know the answer, don't raise your voice to demand it, hoping your tonal volume or your tenacity will magically bring it forth. Instead, do some research. Has your employer done something like this in the past? Will it create a major deviation from policy? Do its costs outweigh its benefits? If you find that your employer is unlikely to give you an item you want, see if you can find an alternative to ask for. It's also a good idea to take an inventory of items in the official company separation agreement that you can trade for others you really need.

## What Do You Have to Do
## to Get What You Want?

There may be certain things that your employer will give you immediately. Others may not be forthcoming. It isn't that your employer can't give them to you; rather, it might take a crowbar or (more to the point) a lawsuit to pry them out of the company.

☞ The question you must ask yourself is *Is this worth my time and effort?* You'll have to decide how far you're willing to go to get what you want.

## What Does Your Negotiating Partner Know About the Situation That You Don't?

This is, by far, the most important question you must answer in order to be sure you'll get what you want. Your negotiating partner knows how far the company will or can go. But you can find out, too. Again, this calls for research. Reread chapter 2 for the details about learning about past practices.

If the positive aspect of negotiating may not accurately be called *winning,* the negative aspect may not be *losing.* If all else fails—you attempt to negotiate and your employer refuses to join you in the dance—you haven't lost. You've tried, which is far better than sitting there helplessly tapping your toes on the sidelines. You've surprised or confounded or possibly only annoyed your partner. Nevertheless, you've moved things a little in the direction you chose. It may be the moment for you to find a more appropriate negotiating partner.

☞ A crucial question you must ask and answer about your negotiating partner is *Does this person have the power to make decisions, or is this person only allowed to read me the company rules?*

If you find your negotiating partner to be only a functionary without decision-making power, find someone else higher up the ladder to work with. Take care not to offend your current negotiating partner. He or she should pass you up the line, saying "I'd recommend we try to help John Doe out here. I just can't." How do you get someone to admit that he or she can't do it because of lack of authority (or nerve, or wisdom)? You say at a crucial juncture in your discussions, *"I'll understand if you must pass on saying 'yes' to my request because it's not the usual thing done around here. Rather than putting you in an awkward position by pressing you to do some-*

*thing you can't, would you direct me to someone who might be able to help me?"*

One of several things may happen: The negotiator will pass you up the line (1) because he or she empathizes with you and wants to help; or (2) because you're a pain in the neck, but he or she won't sabotage you and predispose the folks up the line to feel the same way. In the third scenario, he or she will just say no, and you'll respond in a friendly fashion, *"I'm sorry we disagree here. I'm going to speak with [name of more senior person] about this. I'd be pleased if you'd join me."* If the negotiator won't join you, go ahead and make your appointment to meet with the senior person. (Start that meeting by saying, *"I asked [Mary] to join us, but [she] was unable to meet with us."* Then go ahead and present your issues.) If "Mary" agrees to join you, you've neutralized her, at the very least.

See how the definition of *winning* becomes getting what you want with the least amount of acrimony and the most willing assistance from those around you?

## What Does Your Negotiating Partner Want from the Negotiations?

Your employer wants you out of your job, out of your office, and out of the building so that the company can get on with its business. Your employer also wants to make sure you're reasonably content with your separation package so that you will not surprise the company with a lawsuit or some other retaliatory gesture in the future. And your employer wants this to be done at a price that he or she finds reasonable. This being so, you are assured that for all the important items you consider necessary in your package, your employer wants equally necessary ones. As a negotiating partner, it's your job to satisfy the company that you'll give it what it wants, but in a way that is acceptable to you.

But your next question should be: *What, specifically, does my negotiating partner want?* There may be several things, including some of these:

- A confidentiality statement
- A noncompete, nonsolicit agreement
- A release of discrimination claims, and certainly
- A quiet departure

Review the Release in chapter 10 for some ideas. Once again, research and your personal knowledge of the company will answer the question.

## How Do You and Your Partner Differ as People? How Are You the Same?

These two questions may seem somehow too intimate to affect such an impersonal thing as a termination negotiation. After all, you and your negotiating partner are probably not going to remain fast friends after your sessions are concluded. But there are good reasons for you to be concerned about these things.

Recall the famous scene in *It's a Wonderful Life* in which Jimmy Stewart's character is forced to apply to the town's financial bully and skinflint, Potter, for employment. Potter offers him a chair, and when Stewart sits down, he finds himself almost on the floor, his head just clearing the level of the desktop. This is a crude but effective way for Potter to demonstrate the inequality of their relationship. Jimmy Stewart is begging for work; Potter can supply it, but the price is evident: subservience and capitulation to Potter. While it's doubtful that you'll find yourself staring up from the floor in your negotiations, you may feel as if you are. After all, the company has the power to hire and fire. What power do you have? As we've discussed, you do have power.

☞ The company wants certain things from you, just as you want certain things from the company. They want you to leave quietly. If the person who dispatches you can arrange this, he or she will be perceived as an effective executive. By trading what this person wants for something you want, you'll have heightened his or her regard in the company and gotten what you wanted at the same time. You have real power here.

☞ Negotiations are always personal. The stakes may be argued between employer and employee, but the debate is between you and your partner.

Since this isn't war, make an effort to be friendly. Don't lose your sense of humor while trying to retain your sense of honor. Regard your partner as a person. Once again, do some research to find out about his or her situation and interests. The object of this is not to manipulate your partner, but to level the ground between you. You each want a successful negotiation. Success comes about when the partners to the negotiation feel respect for each other. Ideally, trust and understanding follow. Because of these qualities, great historic treaties have been forged. You're only trying for a separation package. Go for it.

### How Will You Know the Best Way to Make the Right Moves at the Right Time?

Remember that the negotiating table is not Mars; it may be an unfamiliar setting, but it offers the same familiar human challenges you encounter every day in your professional and private life. To be successful at the negotiating table, resolve to hold your temper, keep your focus, and read, understand, and internalize the principles we've put forth in this book.

## HARD WORDS VERSUS SOFT WORDS

Sooner or later in the course of any negotiation, one of the parties is tempted to lash out. This happens when some emotional button is pushed, a toe is stepped on, or a gauntlet is thrown to the floor. Often, the recipient of the supposed insult believes nothing short of a pointed *defense of personal honor* needs to be mounted. But after the shouting ends, and with the negotiations in ruins, the valiant defender of honor concludes that he or she overreacted. Perhaps the defender should have done something differently. But what?

When we vent anger in a negotiation, it's because we have yielded to emotion over reason. It's hard enough to present an objective argument for your own case; the line between you-as-advocate and you-as-client is a fine one. In addition, when you've stated something emotionally, it is the emotion and not the facts of your case that will be responded to. Giving way to emotion will rarely help you get what you want.

The trick to remaining objective and in control of yourself is in your selection of words. It's in your best interest to substitute *soft words* for *hard words*. That is, you'll help your negotiations if you learn to use language driven by your brain, not by your feelings. The sampler below will help you get started.

## Translating Hard Words into Soft Ones

| Hard Words | Soft Words |
|---|---|
| Your separation offer sucks. | This agreement is inadequate, given my years of service here. |
| When I started work, you promised me the moon. You lied. | At the beginning of my employment, commitments were made to me by [name] about the following: [list promises]. I expect that the items that were promised then will be delivered now. |
| I spent thirty of the best years of my life with this company, and this is all you've got to offer me? | I think you'll agree that I've been a tremendous performer. What you've offered isn't commensurate with that performance. |
| I'm listening to your explanations, but I can't make head nor tail of them. I'm not stupid; are you? | I don't understand what you're saying. Please give me a clear reason for your decision. |
| I want a lot more money than you've offered, and I happen to know the company's got it to give. | I expect to be treated in the equitable manner others have been treated. |
| I've spoken to my lawyer and she tells me no problem: I've got enough on you to hang you out to dry! | Although I'd like to settle this amicably, I'm confident that I can and will prevail if this matter is litigated. |
| You expect me to accept this offer on your word alone? Don't make me laugh. Put it in writing. | In order for me to be clear about what you're offering me, I'll need to review it in writing. |

# CONTROLLING THE PACE
# OF NEGOTIATIONS

While we don't believe there are many sneaky negotiating tricks that you should prepare yourself to encounter—or learn to use yourself—there are some tactics that you can use to affect the pace of negotiations. Sometimes you'll want to speed things up or at least keep them moving. At other times, you may want to slow things down. Here are two tactics for these occasions:

*1. The ball is in* **your** *court (keep things moving).*   At the risk of overextending a tennis analogy, "The ball is in your court" refers to something that tennis players know—in order to win the game, they have to return the ball to their opponent. In a hot contest, the return shot is a killer, moving so fast that no mere mortal could return the volley. However, sometimes tennis players just engage in a friendly, low-competition volley—they're hitting the ball so that their partner on the other side of the net *can* return it. The effort is to keep the ball moving—not to score off your opposition.

Applying it to negotiation means that you don't try to score hard points off your negotiating partner. When things get bogged down, agree to disagree for the moment and move on to something easier to discuss. Then return to the more difficult topic when you're less tired and more likely to see the way to compromise.

*2. Paraphrasing (slow it down).*   Paraphrasing is restating what someone else has said, using different words to summarize the point that was made. It's an excellent method of showing that you're listening, because if you can accurately restate what someone else has said, you've obviously heard it the first time around. It's also a way of demonstrating respect, because by listening attentively to the other party, you're showing that you believe his or her view of the situation is important. At the same time, by paraphrasing, you insert an extra sentence into the discussion that temporarily replaces your direct response to what has been said, giving you time to think. It s-l-o-o-o-w-s the dialogue down, without expressly asking for time out. Here's an example:

YOUR BOSS:     Jodie-Beth, if we give you enhanced severance
                pay, we'd leave ourselves open to everyone asking
                for more weeks of severance pay.

YOU:           You're concerned that if you make an exception
                for me, you'd be obligated to do that for everyone
                else?

YOUR BOSS:     Yes.

YOU:           Perhaps there's some way of devising something
                for me that wouldn't leave the company open to
                this problem. Suppose, instead of terming this
                payment "severance," we call it a "special pay-
                ment" and base it on my completion of. . . .

Often, the other person will respond to a paraphrase by nodding or
saying yes. Checking for understanding and acknowledging the other
person's view may seem simple, but they can dramatically change
the tenor and, more important, the pace of the conversation. Practice
a few times on unsuspecting friends and family members—we think
you'll get good results.

Those are the basics of negotiating—no great revelations here, perhaps, but no great mysteries, either.

# 10

# THE STANDARD TERMINATION SETTLEMENT AND RELEASE, DISSECTED

Y ou've completed your negotiations, and you ask yourself, "Am I happy with the result?" If your reply isn't a resounding YES!, don't worry. Popular wisdom suggests that the best negotiations end in an agreement with which neither party is particularly delighted but that both feel they can accept. A good negotiation is a profoundly adult enterprise, with each party forced to respect the other. Only children and the childish get away with claiming, "I want what I want when I want it!"

So now, with the dust settling, your employer reminds you there's that little matter of the Settlement and Release to be executed. *"Oh, sure,"* you say. *"I'll look it over and sign it."* But be careful: You may think your negotiating days are done and you can relax, but you'd be wrong.

## BEFORE YOU SIGN

Employers all too often nestle booby traps into the Settlement and Release that they fail to mention during negotiations *("Oh, didn't I mention your severance would be offset by any compensation you earn over the next six months?")*. Read through your Settlement and Release carefully, thoroughly. You might react to any new provision by taking any of these positions:

146

1.  Had you known your employer would exact this level of concession from you, you would have asked for more. This gives you the opportunity to reopen issues you didn't have the leverage to negotiate the first time around. *Or*
2.  Since you weren't told about a provision during negotiations, it's not going to be part of the Release, *Or*
3.  The provision in the Release is news to you, but if it's so important to the company, who are you to say it shouldn't be included? You just want it set forth in *mutual* terms.

At the end of the day, you are seeking to have your employer modify the objectionable parts of the Settlement and Release, or give you something more by way of consideration. Either way, you'll get what you need.

The standard Settlement and Release used by many employers isn't without its pitfalls, and you must understand what rights you're giving up. The following guide to postnegotiating behavior includes a review of Settlement and Release language and an explanation of the material issues (that is, issues materially affecting the nature of the agreement) and others to look for in all the key clauses.

☞ Unless you have great negotiating skills and a lot of reasons why your company should want you to walk away with a broad smile on your face, you'll be unlikely to get all the concessions outlined below. Be realistic—pick your targets wisely. Decide what's critical to you, and channel your efforts.

## The Settlement and Release Document

| *The Company's Cover Letter* | *Your Thoughts* |
|---|---|

Dear (your name):

| | |
|---|---|
| Due to changing business needs, we have found it necessary to eliminate your position, effective (date). | The reason for terminating you is given as "changing business needs." Is it what you were told or agreed upon? The "effective date" noted is the last day you will report to work. "Reporting to work" doesn't always require your body to appear on your employer's premises. It's the last day you are "employed." |
| You will become eligible for benefits under our Severance Pay Plan, a copy of which is attached, on the date of your position elimination. Any intervening disability will not extend your termination date. According to the Severance Pay Plan, if you sign the attached Release, you will be entitled to receive: | The company is telling you that in the event that you are ill or suffer an accident or injury, you won't be able to prolong your employment by applying for a medical leave of absence. Were you told this during negotiations? Obviously, you can't predict an accident or injury—but is there any medical event that you sought to have covered before your departure? The Family Medical Leave Act mandates that you be given a leave if you apply for it *prior* to being notified that your position has been eliminated. |
| • Severance payments equal to (number) weeks' pay, less withholdings and subject to the following offset. Any severance payments you receive in excess of twelve (12) weeks are offset by income earned in other employment or consulting. You are required to use reasonable efforts to find a position elsewhere. | Were you informed about this employment/consulting offset during your negotiations? (Incidentally, exactly how does your company intend to enforce this? The honor system? Spies? A review of your tax return?) If you didn't discuss this offset during negotiations, it represents a *material* change to your agreement. It discourages you |

| The Company's Cover Letter | Your Thoughts |
| --- | --- |
| | from finding other employment or consulting work to cover the shortfall that arises because your severance dollars reflect only your unadorned base salary. Try to get rid of it, or ask for more in your separation package. |
| • Payout of your unused vacation. Due to your position elimination, the company is departing from its regular policy regarding payout of unused vacation. | Your employer's agreement to pay you for unused vacation days is stated as an exception to the company's usual policy about forfeiture of unused time off—the learning point is that if they can create an exception to the vacation policy because of a layoff, they can create exceptions to other policies as well. You may need to point that out if you are confronted with the *"We-can't-make-exceptions-to-policy"* line in other aspects of your negotiation.
Did you negotiate for payout of unused sick or personal days? The Settlement and Release is silent on these issues. If you did agree to a payout, insert that language here. |
| If you are offered another position by the company prior to your position elimination, you will not become eligible for the company's Severance Pay Plan. | This is an ambiguous statement about alternative employment within the company. Another position? Where? Doing what? At what compensation level? This represents a *material* issue if not agreed to by you during your negotiations. Ask for clarity on the terms of this provision before you agree to it. Suggest the insertion of the words "comparable in salary and status to your former position" after the words *another position*. |

| *The Company's Cover Letter* | *Your Thoughts* |
| --- | --- |

The Release provides that you will not take any legal action against the company arising out of your employment. Section 4 of the Release provides that you have twenty-one (21) days to consider whether you want to sign the Release. You will need to return a signed copy to me twenty-one days from the date of this letter. Your date of termination will not be affected by the date you sign your Release. However, the earlier you return the Release, the earlier the company will be able to provide you with benefits. In addition, Section 6 of the Release advises you to consult with an attorney. Any legal consultation, however, is at your own expense. Signing this Release will not affect your right to obtain unemployment compensation benefits.

This is a key section of the document and will be explored at greater length, below, during the review of the Release itself. One of the significant issues is the number of days you're given to review and sign the Settlement and Release. Under federal law, if you alone are terminated and you are forty years old or older, you must be given twenty-one days to review the Settlement and Release. If you are over forty and are part of a group that is terminated, you must be given forty-five days to review the Settlement and Release. If you are under forty, you'll only need to be given a "reasonable" number of days to review the Settlement and Release. There is no legal definition of what is considered "reasonable."

Most states do not consider severance pay a barrier to the receipt of unemployment benefits. Most states consider salary continuation to *postpone* the date when unemployment compensation begins. You may be eligible for unemployment under either circumstance—lump-sum payments or salary continuation. The key is *when* you can begin to collect your first check.

When you apply for unemploy-ment benefits, the state agency will ask what was the last day you worked—that is, what is the last day you were *paid* for working? The date you provide should be the effective date of your position

| The Company's Cover Letter | Your Thoughts |
| --- | --- |
| | elimination—see above. Your unemployment benefits don't start until you complete a *waiting period* (usually one week) following the last day you received your regular pay. |
| Your health and dental insurance coverage will continue until the end of the month of layoff. You will be sent appropriate COBRA continuation coverage forms that you will need to complete and return within sixty (60) days if you wish to continue coverage beyond your termination date. In general, COBRA allows you to continue your health and dental insurance upon payment of the applicable premium on a month-to-month basis, up to a maximum of eighteen (18) months. All other benefits and coverages will cease on the effective date of your position elimination or layoff. | This is the notice required under federal law, COBRA (Consolidated Omnibus Budget Reconciliation Act of 1986), about health and dental insurance continuation. One of the key aspects of COBRA is that you are permitted to sign up for it any time during the sixty-day period following the receipt of your COBRA notice. Review chapters 7 and 12 regarding health insurance coverage. |
| We value your contribution to the company and wish you the best in your future career endeavors. | Yeah, sure. |
| Sincerely, | |
| (supervisor's name) | |

| Their Separation Agreement and Release | Your Thoughts |
| --- | --- |
| I, [your name], have been employed by the company, or one of its subsidiaries or affiliates ("Employer"). Effective [date], my position is being eliminated. | Again, the reason for your termination is termed a "position elimination." Is this the language you agreed on? |

| *Their Separation Agreement and Release* | *Your Thoughts* |
|---|---|
| Pursuant to the terms of Employer's Severance Pay Plan, if I sign this Release, I am entitled to receive severance pay equal to [number] weeks of pay, less withholdings and deductions ("severance payments"), and my unused vacation. I understand that any payments I receive in excess of twelve (12) weeks are subject to an offset for income earned from employment or consulting work. I agree to use reasonable efforts to find work as a consultant or employee. | This is the "consideration" offered to you for releasing your rights to sue your employer, along with the promise of confidentiality, and perhaps noncompete or nonsolicit promises (see below). Consideration is the value received by you in return for what your company considers to be of value to them. If the consideration outlined doesn't include all the elements you negotiated, have those elements added. Don't accept assurances that those elements will be provided to you outside this agreement. As you'll see below in Section 16, the Settlement and Release states that it represents the *full* agreement of the parties.<br>    This is where the offset against severance for income earned, mentioned above, appears. If this is news to you, see if you can make a trading issue out of it. |
| 1. <u>Release.</u> In exchange for these payments, I agree to release Employer from all claims, demands, actions, or liabilities I may have against Employer of whatever kind, including but not limited to those related to my employment with Employer or the termination of that employment. I agree that this also releases from liability Employer's subsidiaries and affiliated corporations, its affiliates and subsidiaries, its former parents and affiliates of its former parents, and the agents, | This section covers your promises to forgo bringing any lawsuits, claims, actions, etc., of a legal nature against your employer and against all of the companies with which it has an affiliation. The language about releasing its parents, subsidiaries, etc., is very broad. If you are unclear about what companies are included—especially if you've been part of a merger or an acquisition, ask to have the names of the entities covered in this paragraph enumerated. |

| Their Separation Agreement and Release | Your Thoughts |
|---|---|
| directors, officers, employees, representatives, successors, and assigns of such corporations ("those associated with Employer"), whether in their official or individual capacities. I agree that I have executed this Release on my own behalf, and also on behalf of any heirs, agents, representatives, successors, and assigns that I may have now or in the future. | You're also agreeing to release the company against claims brought on your behalf or in your name by your heirs or representatives. |
| I also agree that this Release covers claims under any federal, state, or local statute, regulation, or common law doctrine regarding or relating to employment discrimination, terms and conditions of employment, or termination of employment, including but not limited to the following: Title VII of the Civil Rights Act of 1964, the Civil Rights Act of 1866, the Civil Rights Act of 1991, the Age Discrimination in Employment Act, the Older Workers Benefit Protection Act, the Rehabilitation Act of 1973, the Americans with Disabilities Act, the Employee Retirement Income Security Act of 1974, and all applicable amendments; state human rights or fair employment practices laws; breach of contract, promissory estoppel, or any other contract theory; defamation, employment negligence, or any other tort theory; and rights in any welfare benefit plan or any pension or retirement plan sponsored by Employer. | This important section lists the laws and the types of claims from which you are releasing your employer from liability. Releases are more enforceable by employers when they precisely specify the laws from which they seek release, particularly laws protecting older workers. In addition to releasing the company from actions relating to your termination, you are releasing them from actions taken with respect to your "terms and conditions of employment," which covers a multitude of things, such as your compensation or promotional opportunities. In addition to the federal statutes cited, there is a release of your claims under state law, including the unjust dismissal grounds outlined in chapter 5. Finally, there is a waiver of any claims under any of the company's "welfare" benefit programs, such as pension, profit sharing, or other retirement plans.<br><br>Since this release is very broad, any issues about your employment |

| Their Separation Agreement and Release | Your Thoughts |
|---|---|
| | that you believe might give rise to a lawsuit should be negotiated before you sign this document, or you will lose any opportunity you may have had to assert your rights. |
| I agree that I will never file a lawsuit or demand for arbitration, or institute a claim of any kind, against Employer, or those associated with Employer, including but not limited to claims related to my employment with Employer or the termination of that employment. If I violate this Release by filing a lawsuit or demand for arbitration, or instituting a claim against Employer or those associated with Employer, I agree that I will return all severance payments received pursuant to this Release. I further agree that I will pay all costs and expenses of defending against the suit, arbitration, or claim incurred by Employer or those associated with Employer, including reasonable attorneys' fees. | This provision covers your agreement to return severance and pay attorneys' fees if you, in spite of the Settlement and Release, bring suit against your employer. Notice that the same protection isn't afforded you if the company fails to deliver on its promises. This is an ideal issue for *mutual treatment*—if you sue the company for their failure to abide by the terms of the release, the company will pay your attorney's fees. If the company requires the protection, you want it as well. |
| 2. Continuation Rights. As required by applicable state and federal continuation of coverage laws, I may be eligible to continue certain benefits in accordance with those laws. | This provision relates to your federal COBRA rights and any rights under your state's laws to continue in your former benefits program. See chapters 7 and 12 for a discussion of those laws and your rights. |
| 3. Receipt of Severance Pay. Severance payments will be paid out as soon as administratively feasible after I have received all other payments due me as the result of active employment and | This section informs you of the option of receiving severance pay in a lump sum or as salary continuation. (See chapter 7 for the pros and cons of each method.) |

| *Their Separation Agreement and Release* | *Your Thoughts* |
|---|---|
| the revocation period (explained in Section 5) has expired. Severance payments will be made every two weeks, in the same manner as a payroll check or in a lump-sum payment. If I am rehired by Employer, I agree that I am not entitled to receive severance payments for any period after such rehire. | The section notes that if you are rehired by the company, severance pay stops. This may not be an issue if you plan never to darken the company's door again. In a small industry, with a dominant employer, it may be inevitable that you will return to work for your company—or perhaps for one of its affiliates. If that occurs, your company wants to minimize any windfall represented by the additional severance. Was this discussed during negotiations? It's significant. |
| 4. <u>Period to Consider Signing Release.</u> I have been given a period of twenty-one (21) days to consider whether I want to sign this Release. | Your employer is legally mandated to provide you with time to review the Settlement and Release and seek counsel. The amount of time for this review is determined by your age and whether you are part of a group layoff or are on your own. You could sue the company and the Release would offer the company no protection if the time frame is incorrect. Check the rules outlined on page 150 to be sure that the twenty-one-day period is applicable to your age and termination status. |
| 5. <u>Revocation Period.</u> This Release does not become effective for a period of seven (7) days after it is signed by me, and I have the right to revoke it during that period. Any revocation must be in writing and delivered to [name and address of human resources representative], within the seven- | The revocation period is also required by laws that protect older workers. In effect, even after you sign and return the Settlement and Release, you have an additional seven days to reconsider your decision. Severance payments will stop if you revoke the Settlement and Release. |

| *Their Separation Agreement and Release* | *Your Thoughts* |
|---|---|
| day period. If this person does not *receive* a written revocation by the end of the seven-day period, this Release will become fully enforceable at that time. I understand that if I revoke this Release, I will not be entitled to receive the additional severance payments. | |
| 6. <u>Consulting an Attorney.</u> I acknowledge that I have been advised to consult with an attorney and that any legal consultation will be at my own expense. I have had adequate opportunity to consult with an attorney, and I have read and understand the terms of this Release and am voluntarily signing this Release. | This is certainly an endorsement of the value of the legal profession. Courts have held that employees whose employers advise them to seek legal advice (*Note:* This is at your own expense) can't claim later that their employer took unfair advantage of them. |
| 7. <u>Noncompete and Nonsolicitation</u> (based on whether payment is made in a lump sum or biweekly payments). During "the period in which Employer is making any payments to me" or "the period for which I have received payment," I will not, without the prior written consent of Employer, personally or as an employee or agent of another entity (a) directly or indirectly solicit, divert, or take away, or attempt to solicit, divert, or take away, the business of any person, partnership, company, or corporation with whom Employer, or any subsidiary or affiliated company thereof in which Employer has more than a 20 | A noncompete provision precludes you from working for a competitor or starting a competitive business for some specified period of time. A geographic boundary may also be associated with the provision, permitting you to engage in competitive activity as long as it's outside of the geographic area serviced by your former employer. Courts frown upon clauses that preclude an employee from engaging in his trade or livelihood as a requirement of receiving separation pay. Their reasoning is that the employer is wielding too much control over the negotiation. This, courts feel, approaches restraint of trade. |

| *Their Separation Agreement and Release* | *Your Thoughts* |
|---|---|
| percent equity interest, has established a business or customer relationship, or (b) engage or participate, either individually or as an employee, consultant or principal, partner, agent, trustee, officer or director of a corporation, partnership, or other business entity, in any business in which Employer, including any subsidiary or affiliated company in which Employer has more than a 20 percent equity interest, is engaged. For the one-year period after I cease receiving any payments pursuant to this agreement, I agree that I will not (c) directly or indirectly recruit, induce, or solicit any employee of Employer for employment. During the period in which Employer is making any payments to me pursuant to this Agreement, I will inform any new employer, prior to accepting employment, of the existence of the provisions of this section. | This noncompete clause remains in effect through the period for which severance payments are made. It further requires that the employee not solicit former co-workers to work for his or her new employer for one year following the end of the severance payments or the period covered by severance, if made in a lump sum. It mandates that the employee self-disclose to prospective employers the existence of this provision. |
| | It's probable this noncompete language would survive most courts' scrutiny. It doesn't preclude the employee from engaging in trade forever, or in an overly broad geographic area. It gives the employee the possibility of obtaining the employer's consent to compete in some areas. |
| | Nevertheless, this provision limits your marketability. To get it removed, argue that you're not a threat to the company—perhaps you were terminated for poor job performance, so it's ironic you'd be asked not to compete. Or point out that it's in everyone's best interest that you secure new employment quickly. Be especially careful if you work in a small industry, because this section bans competition against either the employer or its subsidiaries, or against affiliated companies. |
| | The nonsolicitation language addresses your obligation not to induce others from your former |

| *Their Separation Agreement and Release* | *Your Thoughts* |
|---|---|
| | company to come to work with you at your new place of employ. If you had no intention of doing this anyway, you're giving up nothing. But if the reason you'd be attractive to a new employer is your ability to hire others, watch out. Sometimes the most pragmatic way of addressing that problem is to specify that former co-workers who wish to quit and join you may do so. Your employer will likely ask that there be a grace period after you depart before co-workers can join you— the theory is that this grace period will negatively impact your business since your new clients want service immediately. Since indentured servitude is out of the question, your employer recognizes this provision is hard to enforce, anyway. You could just claim that your former co-worker approached you about a new job, even if the truth was just the opposite. |
| 8. <u>Nonadmission of Liability.</u> By entering into this Release, Employer does not admit that it has acted wrongfully with respect to my employment or that I have any rights or claims against Employer. | This paragraph is straightforward. Your employer doesn't want you to use this Settlement and Release as an admission by it that it wronged you. Based on the exhaustive listing of legal rights that you relinquished in Section 1, this provision may be overkill— something like wearing a belt *and* suspenders. Section 11 also relates to nondisclosure obligations— again, it appears redundant. |

| Their Separation Agreement and Release | Your Thoughts |
| --- | --- |
| 9. <u>Confidential or Proprietary Information.</u> I understand that I may not disclose confidential or proprietary information obtained by me during my employment with Employer. | Every company possesses information that is considered fundamental to the business—Coca-Cola isn't the only company that guards its secret formula. That information is termed "confidential" or "proprietary." This section does not define what information is considered proprietary or confidential. If you work in a profession defined by its intellectual work product, you may need to clarify this provision, or it may, in effect, become a noncompete provision precluding you from working in your designated field or profession. |
| 10. <u>Disparaging Remarks.</u> I agree to avoid making any disparaging remarks or taking any actions now, and at any time in the future, that would or could be detrimental in any way to Employer or to any individual employee of Employer, provided, however, that the foregoing shall not restrict my ability to respond to any inquiry from applicable regulatory authorities or to provide information pursuant to legal process. | This section is designed to curb your chattiness in your new employer's executive washroom, your neighbor's cocktail party, or the bullpen at outplacement. The language is both broad and ambiguous. Your first effort should be to have the language removed. You can argue that in the absence of a list of names of every individual employee of the organization, you can't guarantee you won't mistakenly disparage someone. If that argument doesn't cut it, suggest that the language be made mutually applicable—they won't disparage you and you won't disparage them. Since you have more to lose by them disparaging you, this represents a productive compromise. |

| *Their Separation Agreement and Release* | *Your Thoughts* |
|---|---|
| 11. <u>Nondisclosure Provisions.</u> I agree not to disclose to anyone, except my immediate family, accountant, and lawyer any information relating to the existence of this agreement and the subject matter of this agreement, including the dollar amounts set forth, except to the extent required by legal process. Any disclosure to my immediate family, accountant, or lawyer shall be made only upon their agreement not to disclose such provisions to another person. | Your employer doesn't want you to discuss with other employees your separation package— particularly if you were able to obtain concessions. This provision is standard but somewhat unenforceable. The real issue is that your employer doesn't want you to become a source of good information about how you fared during your separation negotia- tions—exactly the kind of person we recommended you find the moment you thought your own job was in jeopardy. Our advice is that it's foolish to brag to people about your negotiating acumen. You know you did well; feel *quietly* proud. |
| 12. <u>Future Cooperation.</u> I agree to reasonably cooperate with Employer, its financial and legal advisers, or government officials in connection with any business matters in which I was involved or any existing or potential claims, investigations, administrative proceedings, lawsuits, and other legal and business matters that arose during my employment with Employer, as reasonably requested by Employer. Related and custo- mary travel and accommodation expenses will be reimbursed by Employer in accordance with its policies and procedures. | This cooperation section can be beneficial to you if you suspect that you might serve as a key witness in litigation pending against your employer. Ask your employer if there's a particular situation that the company believes involves you. If they mention something that you didn't take into account when you negotiated your separation pay package, this provision gives you an opportunity to remind your employer that they are requesting you to testify on the company's behalf. *Favorably* testify on the company's behalf. Helpfully, even. Some companies make a practice of deposing about-to-be- terminated employees so that the record is preserved. These |

| Their Separation Agreement and Release | Your Thoughts |
|---|---|
| | companies are not suggesting anything as unsubtle as, *"We're afraid once you leave this place, you'll tell the truth and sink us"* or *"We're afraid once you leave this place you'll lie your mouth off on the witness stand."* If the company doesn't suggest it, you might suggest that someone in the law department take your deposition before you leave. That cooperation, of course, will have to be repaid in your settlement package. |
| 13. <u>Employment Inquiries.</u> I will direct all employment inquiries to the Human Resources Department. In the event that the Employer's Human Resources Department receives such inquiries about me, Employer shall respond solely by giving my dates of employment and last position held. This paragraph shall not restrict Employer's ability to provide complete information with respect to my employment when expected to do so under applicable law, rules, or regulatory requirements. | Identifying who will be responsible for responding to employment inquiries made about you may be an entirely routine matter, or a highly sensitive one. If you parted company with your employer as part of a straightforward layoff, on good terms with your former supervisor, and without raising any legal issues, this provision should be a no-brainer. Let the Human Resources Department do its job so you don't lose any sleep. |
| | If your departure was less than amicable, or if it was complicated, you should include in your negotiations the identity of the person who will provide references for you. This section should state what the person will say and how you will be compensated if this section is violated and you are damaged. Since it's difficult to prove the source of the gossip that always accompanies a sensitive |

| *Their Separation Agreement and Release* | *Your Thoughts* |
|---|---|
| | termination, or that maliciously motivated blackballing is occurring, your effort is less to control what is said—since you may never be able to track who said it—and more to warn your employer that you will make a nuisance of yourself if they don't make an effort to button loose lips. |
| 14. <u>Outplacement.</u> Employer has retained [name of company] to assist me in my career transition, by providing me with outplacement counseling services. These services are designed to assist me by providing me with counseling on resume writing, interviewing skills, networking techniques, and a job-search campaign. | Outplacement exists to help both you and your employer. It gets you off the premises and into the arms of a trained counselor, skilled at helping turn your grief and anger into a productive search for new employment.<br><br>If you can't convert outplacement services into cash, there's no reason to refuse the service—free long distance calls to your Mom! —and every reason to learn what you can from them. Don't, however, confuse the outplacement counselor with your friend or a trusted professional hired by you. Anything you say about your former employer can and will be repeated.<br><br>And, as advised previously, don't vacate your office on the promise that the view from the outplacement office will leave you breathless and satisfied until your separation negotiations are complete. Lingering on-site gives you the opportunity to access your allies, should the need arise. |
| 15. <u>Rights to Benefits.</u> My rights to benefits under any employee benefit plans in which I am | This section is benign if you've done your homework. It says that any information about your |

| Their Separation Agreement and Release | Your Thoughts |
|---|---|
| currently enrolled and which are not specifically addressed in this document will be determined in accordance with the terms of such plans. My rights to benefits under such plans and programs shall be governed by applicable law and by the terms of the plans, which may be modified or terminated at any time. | benefits not contained in this agreement is covered by the Plan Descriptions for those programs. If you've agreed to have your benefits treated in a standard fashion, and you understand the implications of what the term "standard" means, this section is innocuous. However, if you've negotiated something special or extra under a plan, you'll want it spelled out here. Otherwise, the signing of this document may waive whatever special treatment you've negotiated. Your operating philosophy should be: *If it's not stated in writing in this document, it doesn't exist.* |
| 16. <u>Entire Agreement.</u> I have signed this Release with the understanding that this is the entire agreement between me and Employer relating to my employment and my termination from employment. This Release includes all prior discussions and agreements between me and Employer. I acknowledge that this Release cannot be changed except by writing signed by both me and Employer. | This section eliminates your claim that a concession that was agreed upon during the negotiations has, due to administrative or other oversight, not been included here. Remember, don't accept promises that the situation will be handled outside of this agreement. You want it spelled out in the Settlement and Release. |
| 17. <u>Enforceability.</u> In case any part of this Release shall be invalid, or unenforceable for any reason, the validity, legality, and enforceability of the remaining provisions shall not in any way be affected or impaired. | This language gives the company an out in the event the law changes, rendering some language in the document unenforceable. Often, it's used when a noncompete or nonsolicitation clause is found by a court to be too broad. |

| *Their Separation Agreement and Release* | *Your Thoughts* |
|---|---|
| 18. <u>Governing Law.</u> This Release will be construed and interpreted in accordance with the laws of [name of state]. | This language, like the enforceability language, gives your employer some certainty as to which state's law will be used in the event of a dispute. There is a possibility that you may have a choice of law if you live in one state but work in another. If you recall the state law chart in chapter 5, your ability to bring an unjust dismissal case varies considerably. For example, if you were an employer whose operations are in New York (a conservative state), but you employ people who live in New Jersey (a liberal state), you'd specify that New York law would control. Obviously, as the employee, you'd want the opposite. |

Now, here's how to proceed: Read your Settlement and Release carefully. Make notes about the changes necessary. Review the Settlement and Release and your notes with an attorney, if you require assistance. Return to your employer and reopen negotiations, if appropriate. Sign the Settlement and Release only after you're satisfied you've negotiated as effectively as you can for the things that are important to you.

# 11

# BUT WHAT ABOUT
# MY CASE?

S o much for the game plan and the pieces you want to capture. But what about the specifics? How will you deal with the unique problems in your individual separation negotiations?

Actually, the majority of problems confronted in a separation negotiation have been confronted and successfully resolved. Among these are common situations and perhaps not-so-common ones. To tie up any loose ends, let's review these problems and their tactical resolutions.

Q  Suppose my employer expressly acknowledges that my supervisor was wrong and I was legally harmed when I was terminated. Does this affect my separation package negotiations?

A  You bet. You could ask to be reinstated to your old job. Your decision will reflect whether you still want to work with this company or you believe that it's time to move on, taking a *really, really, really* good separation package with you. If you decide it's time to leave, in addition to the negotiating strategies we've outlined in previous chapters, you can ask to be compensated in order to remain *completely* whole during the period prior to obtaining new employment. This means you are requesting full pay and benefits as though you had never been terminated. If any of your future benefits are adversely affected by your precipitous departure, obtain make-whole compensation as income protection. For example, by being terminated, your pension will be diminished since you won't be around to earn additional years of contributions; your 401(k) may not vest in contributions made by your employer. Cash compensation today should offset those shortfalls. If the behavior exhibited by your employer was particularly obnoxious, seek compensation based on the stress to which you were subjected and the potential embarrassment to the company, were the matter to become public. Be politely aggressive but realistic.

You were terminated, so we recommend you plan on leaving. Staying with this company for just an apology, even though they've done the noble thing by confessing their sins, would probably be a big mistake (as we discussed in chapter 8). On the other hand, leaving without everything you would have had in the absence of your termination would also be a big mistake. Suing to collect from the company is never the best alternative (see chapter 5). So, get what you're looking for from the company through a *negotiated* departure. We suggest you consult with an attorney so that you don't shortchange yourself.

**Q** My boss has been a real bastard to me. I'd like to really embarrass him on my way out. What can I do?

**A** Forget revenge, at least the down-and-dirty, low-road kind. You'll need to elicit at least *minimum* goodwill from your boss in order to successfully negotiate your separation. Humiliate your boss now, and he won't recover from it in time to make a good negotiating partner. Instead, minimize your boss's control over you by involving others in the negotiation. Do it politely, and don't slam doors behind you. You never know (particularly in a small industry) when you'll meet and perhaps need the goodwill of someone again. If your boss really was a jerk, your style and elegance will visibly contrast with his boorishness. Take the high road and win! Winning, as we've said, is the best revenge.

**Q** I'm in what I think is a great situation—I anticipated that I was going to be terminated and found another job. After I resigned, my company made me a counteroffer that's better than the offer made by the new employer. Should I accept it?

**A** The old thinking held that accepting a counteroffer was the career equivalent of suicide. They sweet-talk you today to stay, but nail you in six months when you're least prepared—and you're sitting there without anyplace left to go. This probably still holds true if you've been fired and you've somehow persuaded your employer to let you stay on—you're an accident looking for a place to happen. A resignation followed by a counteroffer, however, is different in today's work environment.

It's clear that the old ties of loyalty in business are a thing of the past. Most employers neither expect nor demand lifetime loyalty from their employees. You know your company better than anyone—can it be trusted to make you a counteroffer because it sincerely wants to keep you? To make the best decision, ask yourself these questions: Are your skills unique and valuable? Is your employer likely to hold a grudge? Are you marketable in the event that you'll need to leave in six months? Is your head so far out the door and into your new job or just leaving the old place that there's really no point in staying? Your decision should be based on your honest answers to these questions. Since you're talking to yourself here, be honest and forthright.

**Q**  I decided to beat them to it and found a new job before they could fire me. How should I tell them?

**A**  Gracefully. Give your employer a *brief* letter that says you've been offered an opportunity that you just couldn't pass up, and your decision to leave was made carefully. Don't elaborate on your new job's benefits or promises to the detriment of those offered by your old employer. If it's true, state that you enjoyed working for your company. Provide two weeks notice, which is the norm, and specify your last day of employment. Extended notice is usually a bad idea—you want to leave, and in most cases, your employer has accepted your decision and wants to get your replacement up to speed as soon as possible. If you're asked to stay on to train your replacement or finish a project, do so for a reasonable time. Don't let it jeopardize your start date at your new job.

**Q**  I resigned and gave two weeks' notice. My employer told me to leave immediately. Have I been fired?

**A**  No. But be sure you've written—and kept a copy of—your letter of resignation. It documents the action. Should the references provided to prospective employers state something else, your employer's in trouble.

Employees who voluntarily resign are not eligible for unemployment compensation in most states unless they can prove "constructive discharge." Constructive discharge means that your employer's behavior was so awful that your decision to resign was not made freely—your employer's behavior, in effect, gave you no alternative but to resign. If your resignation is converted to a termination by your employer's failure to accept reasonable notice (two weeks is reasonable, two years is not) and you don't start work for a new employer immediately, you may be eligible for unemployment benefits. Check with your state's Department of Labor, Unemployment Insurance Division. You'll find it in your telephone book under state government listings.

**Q**  I've been at my company for only six months. Yesterday, I was told that I'm being terminated with two weeks pay. I really don't have anyone up the line who will stand up for me—I'm too new. What should I do?

**A**  You're obviously not in the same position as someone who has been with the company for years and built up a lot of IOUs. But, you still have three potential allies: an executive recruiter (if one placed you in your job), the hiring manager (if that isn't the person who fired you), and someone in human resources whom you know or who is reputed to be fair. The executive recruiter may be particularly sympathetic to your plea if you work in a concentrated industry or you're a potential hiring manager in the future. Executive recruiters don't want their reputations sullied, either, and your employer's precipitous action makes the recruiter look bad. In the absence of a mentor or other powerful allies, these people are your best bets. If the following is a true description of your situation, use it in your argument to your boss: You were recruited away from another employer where, based on your greater tenure, had you been fired you would have received much more severance. Imply that representations were made to you at the time of hiring that induced you to leave your former company. This may get you some additional consideration—or even a lot more consideration, depending on what was said to you at the time of hiring.

Q I'm one of the lucky ones. I was given notice of my termination last Friday. On Monday I met an old friend for lunch, and by the end of the lunch, I had signed on with her company—with an increase in salary. I want to collect the separation package that my former employer alluded to during our Friday meeting. What do I do?

A You need to expedite the discussions with your old company. The standard argument for a separation package is that you will be unfairly damaged if you leave without a compensation cushion. You'll be out there, the reasoning goes, pounding the pavement, feverishly scanning the help-wanted ads, looking for a job. If you have a new job to go to immediately, your damages will be considered mitigated. If your present employer is aware of the situation, the company may try to get away with offering you the most minimal package. Get moving. Tell your employer you're shocked by the news of your termination, but you want to get on with your life. Set a date and declare your objective to be gone by that date, with all the ink dry on the necessary paperwork. Also, ask your friend for a little slack—see if she can give you a few weeks to tie up the loose ends at your former place of work.

Q My separation negotiations with my employer have just started, and they've told me they need my office for my successor. They've offered me an extensive outplacement package that includes office and secretarial support. Should I move now?

A No, no, a thousand times no. Don't leave until you conclude your negotiations for your separation package. You may need a number of people to help argue your cause. The last thing you want is to be out of sight and out of mind. If you're sitting there looking brave, you'll increase the guilt factor (which can work in your favor), and you'll retain face-to-face access to people who might otherwise dodge your phone calls.

Our theory has always been that outplacement offices were invented so that employers could rid themselves of ex-employees who had become, by circumstance, eyesores. Don't agree to be moved down the hall, into a cubicle, or anywhere else. Instead, act normally. Show up for work on time and go to your office. If you're asked why you won't give up your office, say that unless someone knows otherwise, you expect your separation negotiations to be fast and amicable. Challenge your employer to say otherwise.

**Q** I'm going nuts. My boss has treated me like dirt for the last two years. I can't be in the same room with him without my skin breaking out in a blotchy rash. I know you advocate bringing counsel in only as a last resort, but I can't take another minute. What do I do?

**A** Turn it over to an attorney now and let him or her handle it. While we encourage you to assert your rights, we don't recommend that you do it at the risk of your mental health. Hire counsel to do the job—let him or her get on with it on your behalf. Never fear: your attorney will remind the company of your dermatologist's bills.

**Q** It's clear to all concerned that my boss discriminated against me. The company wants to settle this fast and my attorney is going to meet with them next week. Should I be there?

**A** No. Having turned the matter over to an attorney, let him or her earn the fee. Attorneys know that the information they learn during negotiations, while not confidential and privileged, should be maintained with discretion. If you're there, the company will be less forthright about their wrongdoing. That means negotiations will take longer. Take the afternoon off and relax. Your attorney will call you when the meeting is over.

**Q** Suppose I have absolute evidence that my company has discriminated against me, but my separation package discussions are going really well. Have I made a mistake if I fail to say something about this evidence?

**A** Yes. If discussions between you and the company break down and you end up in litigation, you may be asked whether you raised your legal claim during negotiations. You'll want to answer in the affirmative.

There are gentle ways of raising the legal issue even as things are proceeding smoothly—perhaps somewhere along the way, you "confide" in a human resources person that you're relieved things are going well because you didn't want to have to bring suit against a company that had, for the most part, treated you well. You might quietly offer to perform an "exit interview" at the close of negotiations. (Before doing this, be sure you've received your separation paycheck, and that the check has cleared the bank.) If you have the ability to alert the company to a systemic problem about which they are unaware, you'll be doing the company and your former co-workers a service, and you'll have raised the legal problem with style and assurance.

**Q** I have an employment contract. Does that change any of your advice about negotiating my separation pay package?

**A** Yes. If your employer thinks highly enough of you to provide you with a contract (and the pay that usually accompanies one), you should immediately treat yourself to the advice of counsel. The interpretation of the contract is probably best left in the hands of the people who draft these things for a living. Issues should be raised and resolved quickly by your attorney.

**Q** My boss is a low-life jerk. I've been secretly tape-recording our meetings. Is this a useful thing to do?

**A** State laws differ about what a party to a taped conversation must do in order to follow the law or to have the tape admitted as evidence in court. Since the range of requirements for legal taping is fairly broad (both parties must know and agree, or the taping party must include a "beeping" noise at periodic intervals, or only one party needs to know and consent, and so on), you'll need to be aware of your own state's laws.

In a moral or ethical sense, it's clear that taping without the other party's consent isn't honorable. How would you feel if your employer did it to you without your knowledge? On the other hand, if you catch your employer saying something really awful, and you've got it on tape, you can bet it will expedite the negotiation.

**Q** I understand that my attorney should only show his face after I've taken the negotiations as far as I can. But, should I allude to his counsel during my discussions with my employer?

**A** Do it subtly. Lawyers talk "attorney speak." Read chapter 5 on employment law and use your new vocabulary. Speak as you've been coached—that's what this book is all about. Sound confident and well prepared. In addition, you might read over chapter 9 on negotiating using "soft words."

**Q**  My mentor has been great during some tense separation negotiations with the human resources department. We've agreed on almost all the terms, except that we can't come to closure about my stock options. Should I go back to my mentor for help?

**A**  Yes. Tell your mentor that you've ironed out all the terms—except for one that only she is powerful enough to affect. Don't be shy—now is the time to ask your mentor for assistance.

**Q**  You've alluded to hiring an attorney several times. What if I can't afford one?

**A**  That's why we wrote this book. You may wish to consider finding an attorney who will work with you on a contingency basis (see chapter 6, which covers the fee structure used by counsel). Or, if the amount that you hope to negotiate and obtain from your employer may not justify hiring counsel, find someone whose good sense and judgment you respect to help you execute your strategy to get your separation package increased. This person should be capable of giving you moral and intellectual support— a shoulder to cry on, and a good head above those shoulders. Do not consult a co-worker. Follow the advice in this book and adapt the strategies outlined for your particular situation. We predict you'll make yourself proud.

**Q**  What do you recommend as negotiating strategies for improving a layoff separation package?

**A**  The easiest part about discussing a layoff separation package is that the blame for the termination will be placed on external factors—a merger, a product failure, an unprofitable business division—and not on you or your actions. Since you aren't the cause of the problem, you're well positioned to argue for a generous separation package.

   The hardest part of improving a layoff separation package is, with greater numbers of people being terminated, decisions involving who is being selected for layoff and what they will be given will have undergone greater administrative scrutiny. Your company may assert in a layoff that the separation package has been crafted for the multitudes and that enhancing the package for one individual will leave the company open to a charge of discrimination. Your objective is to separate yourself from the others being laid off so that you can "de-couple" your separation package. Use arguments about timing and tenure. (See chapter 7 for a fuller explanation.)

**Q** What do you recommend as negotiating strategies for improving a firing separation package?

**A** Don't be overly vocal when making known your many contributions to the company's success over the years. That will only invite a debate about your job performance. Remove from the hands of your boss (who may dislike you), or from a lower-level human resources person (who may lack the authority to make an exception on your behalf) the exclusivity of making decisions about your fate. Do this by bringing others into the negotiations—senior managers or vocal peers. Use your contacts assertively. If necessary, remind others that "fault" is a two-way street. See chapter 8 for more details.

**Q** My boss is impossible—either he lacks the authority to cut a deal with me (*"I'll have to check on that . . ."*), or he's trying for a win-lose scenario and won't be satisfied until I lose. What should I do?

**A** If you're satisfied that there is no possibility of success by negotiating with your boss, and you're willing to risk antagonizing him in order to get the result you want, go around or above him. Tell his boss or human resources that your boss's personal antagonism is getting in the way of the *company* achieving what it wants—a fast and fair separation package. Ask that someone else be assigned to work with you. And don't allow your boss to be the person who issues your official references from the company.

**Q** How long should the negotiations take? I'm afraid mine are going on too long and everyone's losing patience.

**A** Or interest, which is the greater risk. While there's no hard-and-fast rule, if your negotiations take longer than two months, your promise to sue will lose its power—just one more case on the company's litigation docket. Tell your employer, *"This has been going on too long. Let's reach agreement within the next five days."* And in a friendly but forceful fashion, put pressure on your allies to help you get there. Use your contacts—tell them you're under pressure from your family "and others" to resolve this amicably. Intimate that there's a barracuda-esque attorney hovering in the wings. That ought to do it.

**Q**  I'd like to take everything out of here when I leave—my work, my files, the kitchen sink. What do you advise?

**A**  Don't. Take only what belongs to you—which doesn't include the product you created on behalf of your former employer. Don't be anxious about leaving your favorite creation behind. If you thought of it once, you're capable of improving it. In any event, be careful. If you're covered by any confidentiality or proprietary work product policies, your employer can hang you if you steal or if you reveal sensitive information to a competitor.

Can you be expected to wipe your memory clean? That's unrealistic, and your new employer is obviously hiring you based on your significant professional experience. But don't make it too simple for your prior employer to track you down by following the trail generated by company files that are missing.

Having said this, be sure that you have certain things in your possession before you give up any office documents related to your employment history. You may need these should you contemplate legal action against your employer, or even if you're only playing it safe against possible problems in the future. See chapter 2 for a list.

**Q**  I hesitate to get into negotiations. I don't have much experience as a negotiator and I'm afraid that my supervisor or human resources person, who, I suspect, is a skilled negotiator, will back me into a corner with negotiating "tricks." Is this a real problem?

**A**  The human resources people would be ecstatic if they thought you believed they were negotiating magicians.

However, there are two cardinal rules that you must be aware of, and that you ignore only to your detriment. Rule Number One: Listen, and don't say anything until you're sure you understand what you're agreeing to. Rule Number Two: Protect yourself by saying to your employer's proposals, *"Interesting thought. I'll get back to you with a response after I've given it more consideration."* Repeat this as often as you need to. Don't be concerned about feeling clueless at the moment when an unexpected issue is raised or a possible remedy offered. Don't get angry, don't get scared, and don't agree to anything until you decide it's in your best interest to do so. Gather all those issues that you don't have an answer to then and there, thank the person for a productive conversation, schedule the next meeting, and leave. Then, go to whomever you've been working through your issues with—your attorney, spouse, dog—decide how you want to respond, and go back to the discussions informed and prepared. Dirty tricks are impossible when you're in control.

**Q** I'm afraid that, once we've negotiated and I've walked out the door, the company will find ways to delay paying out the money we've agreed on. I know people this has happened to. How can I stay on top of the company about this?

**A** The best way to stay on top of this situation is to do it in writing. Not by issuing threats or demands, but by writing friendly, cordial, even warm letters—letters that nevertheless perform a crucial function. They create records that can be called upon later, if necessary. Sometimes, an employer will be reluctant to commit to exact time frames in writing. That's okay. You should confirm your understanding in a written thank-you note. If your employer does not challenge your understanding, it's reasonable to assume you are in agreement. The note might be written this way:

Dear [*your boss*]:

Thanks for meeting with me on [*date*] to conclude our separation discussions. I really appreciate all the time you've put into working this out.

Based on your statements, I expect to receive my final paycheck on [*date*], my 401(k) payment on [*date*] and [*etc., etc.*].

Thanks again for all your help in resolving this matter to everyone's satisfaction.

Cordially,

[*you*]

Now the burden is on your employer to tell you if your letter contains any inaccuracies. If they don't perform as they agreed to, first make a cordial telephone call, then follow it up in writing. If there's a big delay, express your concern and disappointment in writing. If necessary, take your well-documented paper trail to an attorney, particularly if it involves ERISA plans (retirement programs—see chapter 7) or if the amount in contention is small, try going to small claims court on your own. (The court will give you filing instructions.)

**Q**   Why do you place so much emphasis on assembling your allies? Doesn't that just involve a whole bunch of people in your termination, a matter that is better kept quiet?

**A**   Your termination is not a blot on your character that should only be discussed in hushed tones. If you can go it alone, great. But you may need your allies' support and help, which you will likely get if you ask for it.

In most instances, the person who notified you of your termination was either your immediate supervisor or someone from human resources. The former may have selected you for termination; the latter's authority is prompted by policy. Your goal is to bring pressure on the person with whom you are negotiating to sweeten your deal. You need to find people who like you or your work to argue your cause. The more powerful your supporters are—either they outrank your boss or they bring in revenue—the greater their influence. Similarly, if you are negotiating with someone from human resources, you want influential business people to argue that human resources policy is not a constraint—it's the minimum, not the maximum you should be offered.

You will then play one against the other—seeking outside intervention whenever you reach a stalemate in the discussions. In effect, the company is not negotiating with you, they're negotiating among themselves on your behalf. Your role is to keep people actively involved in intervening on your behalf by presenting compelling reasons for them to improve your package.

**Q**   If we've negotiated my termination but I find language in the release that wasn't there in the negotiations, what do I do?

**A**   Tell them that this language is news to you, and ask them what happened. If they insist that the language must stay, you can do one of three things: (1) If the new language binds you to some behavior (such as conforming to a confidentiality provision), insist that the same provision be binding on the company (mutuality). (2) If the language would have you give up a legal right (for example, the right to sue the company), insist that the company offer you something of value in exchange. (3) If you find the offensive language untenable, you can refuse to sign the agreement. In that case, the deal will probably be off and your only recourse will be to take legal action. Review chapter 5 for further ideas.

**Q**   I know that my boss has been trying to get up the courage to terminate me. We've already met twice, but she hasn't been able to come straight out with it. Should I get it over with and ask her if she's telling me I'm fired?

**A**   No! She may have trouble using the "F" (for "Fired") word, but she'll probably have no trouble answering yes to the question, "Am I fired?" Wait her out, and get your act in gear during this hiatus.

**Q**   My boss is a hothead. I've heard that when he terminates people, he enjoys verbally abusing them, too. If I ever get into that situation, what should I do?

**A**   Don't respond to the abuse in either anger or fear. Say nothing and walk out the door. Better still, ask his assistant to come in to be a witness of his abusive behavior.

**Q**   If I'm taking notes during my termination meeting and someone asks me why I'm doing it, what do I say?

**A**   Tell them this: "*As you will understand, this is an emotional situation for me, and I want to be sure I'm getting down what is said so that I can review it when I have a chance to be reflective.*" Remember, keep note-taking during the meeting to a minimum; listen and remember what is said. Make notes after the meeting is over.

**Q**  If I go to human resources and ask to see my personnel file, what do I answer if I'm asked why I want to see it?

**A**  Answer that you make it a habit to check the information in your file periodically in order to be sure that it's up-to-date. Or tell them that you're applying for a mortgage, or you want to review your beneficiaries, or anything else that makes sense based on the information that can be found in your file.

**Q**  If I've made a friend in human resources, how do I find out from him what exceptions have been made to the company's separation policy?

**A**  Ask how much latitude you or your manager or some other executive might have to make exceptions to the policy. Is the policy the same in all situations? If not, what are the exceptions?

**Q**  How do I ask my mentor and other friends in the company to support me during my separation talks?

**A**  Call them and set up a time to meet. Explain your situation and ask them for their perception of what is going on. Then ask them if they are positioned to help you. If they say yes, be specific about what you'd appreciate them doing for you; for example, *"Please call my boss and remind him that you, as our largest client, always felt my work was great, so please give [your name] whatever additional consideration you can in her exit package."*

# PART FOUR

# POST-TERMINATION

# 12

# NOW, WHAT DO I DO WITH THIS STUFF?

Consider your insurance and benefits, which until your termination were managed for you by your employer. That was probably a comfortable arrangement, and you might have developed a "these things will take care of themselves" attitude, but it's time for you to take control. Once your employment ends, the status of your insurance and benefits changes. It's up to you—*only* you—to handle these matters from now on.

## TYPES OF INSURANCE YOU'LL NEED TO REPLACE

Most employees are covered by one or more of three types of insurance:

- Health insurance and other medical coverage
- Life insurance
- Long-term disability insurance

## REPLACING INSURANCE

Your initial consideration will be obtaining medical coverage. If you don't obtain medical coverage through a new employer, your first effort should always be to examine your working spouse's benefits program—assuming you have a spouse who's working for a company that provides health care coverage. Your next effort should be to consider your former employer's health continuation plan, which may be mandated by federal or state law. Finally, you may consider purchasing an individual policy.

The good news goes downhill from there. All the other insurance you carried though your employer, such as life and disability, will end unless your employer extends your coverage under the company's group plan or if there's an individual conversion policy offered through the insurance company. If there isn't, you may need to secure your own insurance. Your concern should center on time and money, since you may not have much of either to spare. Having to find a job is stressful enough; having to find and buy insurance just compounds your fears (*"Suppose I never find a job? Suppose I get hit by a truck? Suppose I get hit by a truck while trying to find a job?"*). Even under the best of circumstances (that is, not the ones you're under at the moment) a "peace-of-mind" purchase of insurance for an event that you don't even want to picture elicits some hostility. Usually, you feel as if you've just swallowed the bait.

With that lure in mind, here are some practical questions to ask yourself about replacing insurance:

- How's your health? If you can't continue your participation through your ex-employer's plans and you don't have a spouse or a spouse's plan to join, examine whether you *need* the insurance. Move faster if your health's not good, slower if it's okay. Even if you want coverage, can it wait until you are hired by your next employer?
- If you need it, and it can't wait until you join your next employer, what are the best sources for purchasing reasonably priced coverage?

## Health Insurance and Other Medical Coverage

Retaining health insurance or other medical coverage may be the most critical aspect of your negotiations with your former employer. If you or a member of your family requires ongoing and expensive medical treatment, you won't be able to afford *not* to have the coverage. Because of the exclusion of coverage for existing medical conditions under many new employers' medical plans, you may need an interim policy (either before the effective date of the Health Insurance Portability Act or because that law's provisions relating to credit for prior coverage still leaves you without complete coverage).

*COBRA.* Under the 1986 federal law, the Consolidated Omnibus Budget Reconciliation Act (COBRA), employers of more than twenty employees must offer health and medical continuation coverage to terminated employees and their dependents. While COBRA has its downsides, it's far preferable to having no coverage at all. Your cost will likely increase considerably, because your employer is allowed to pass on to you the administrative costs along with the premium charges in full—the premium you were paying as an employee along with any amounts paid by your employer as a subsidy to you. You will be paying 102 percent of the total cost, unless you are able to negotiate with your employer for something else. Also, you must exercise your right to purchase COBRA coverage within sixty days of notification in writing by your employer. And employees who are terminated for certain kinds of misconduct are ineligible for COBRA.

In general, COBRA coverage extends for eighteen months, but can be provided to your dependents for up to thirty-six months if there's been a divorce or a child has lost dependent status. In addition, effective January 1, 1997, the eighteen months' coverage can be extended for up to twenty-nine months for you or your dependents who are disabled at any time during the first sixty days of continuation coverage. However, your former employer can charge you for 150 percent of the applicable premium during the eleven-month extension.

If you obtain employment elsewhere, your new employer can't exclude you or a member of your family from coverage because of a preexisting condition for a period of more than twelve months—eighteen months for late enrollees—a period that must be reduced by the length of prior continuous coverage, unless that prior coverage was followed by a period of no coverage of sixty-three days or longer.

If there are fewer than twenty employees in your company, you may be eligible for comparable insurance continuation mandated under state law for smaller employers. The table on page 184 lists states that have such laws.

## States with Health Care Continuation Laws

| Alabama | Maine | North Carolina | South Dakota |
|---|---|---|---|
| Connecticut | Maryland | North Dakota | Tennessee |
| Georgia | Massachusetts | Ohio | Texas |
| Illinois | Minnesota | Oklahoma | Vermont |
| Iowa | Nebraska | Pennsylvania | West Virginia |
| Kansas | New Hampshire | Rhode Island | Wisconsin |
| Kentucky | New Mexico | South Carolina | |

Be alert to situations in which one spouse is eligible for your company's retiree medical coverage (if your employer offers it, since it is usually less expensive than COBRA and doesn't have the eighteen-month time limitation) or Medicare COBRA *and the other spouse isn't eligible.* You may need to do one thing to provide coverage for yourself and another to provide coverage for your spouse. You should also be concerned about the consequences to your coverage when a dependent child is no longer carried by your health insurance, an event sometimes triggered by the child's age—eighteen, twenty-one, or twenty-five. Other policies end dependent status when a child graduates from school. Similarly, adult dependent children may be treated differently under COBRA than under your former plan. Know what your COBRA options encompass.

As we suggested in chapter 7, if you don't immediately move to a new job, it's in your best interests to negotiate with your employer to remain in your group plan for as long as possible before having to purchase COBRA coverage. If you can persuade your employer to continue to subsidize your premium so that you pay only a reduced amount, so much the better.

***Individual Health Care Policies.*** If you're not eligible for COBRA or state law continuation coverage, you exhaust your COBRA coverage, or you become self-employed, effective July 1, 1997, you are guaranteed the right to purchase an individual policy at a rate that is no higher than the premiums charged to someone who is purchasing the same policy and is in good health.

If you decide to purchase an individual policy, check with an insurance broker about your range of options. For example, if you become a consultant, you may be able to have your business covered under a group plan. Or you can purchase a plan with a large deductible and, in effect, self-insure except for disasters. Or while you may have enjoyed an indemnity plan that allowed you to use the services of any doctor of your choice, a managed care plan may prove to be less costly, although your choice of caregivers will be restricted.

HMOs will take individual subscribers, but will limit your choice of physician to their own network providers. The benefits of HMOs are that they're fairly stable, they tend to remain in business, and they have no caps on usage, other than network restrictions. The charge for each visit to an HMO is also limited to a small copayment by you, instead of the customary 20 percent to 35 percent of the medical fee you paid while covered by an indemnity plan (20 percent to 35 percent of the medical fee, that is, *provided* you had satisfied your insurance deductible).

*Dental Insurance.* Dental insurance, which is offered by a large number of employers, is also covered by COBRA and is extremely costly to purchase on an individual basis. Your best bet is to stick with COBRA, followed by the conversion plan offered through your employer's carrier following the expiration of your COBRA coverage if you don't have other options.

*Health Care Coverage through Associations.* Many professional groups and clubs offer health care programs to their membership. The cost and the quality of these plans vary, so do some checking. Practically, association plans may be less expensive than an individual plan obtained through an insurance broker. Conversely, the association's plans will rarely be as good as a company group plan, because membership in associations tends to be transient. The people who remain in the association's plan do so because they have no choice—they can't obtain insurance elsewhere. This results in the plan having either higher cost or reduced coverage.

## Life Insurance

Unlike health care coverage continuation, which may be mandated by COBRA or your state law, there are no laws requiring the extension of life insurance. If you don't negotiate for an extension, it's

likely the *group* life plan you have through your employer will end
on your termination date.

Often, an *individual* policy may be purchased through your
employer's insurance carrier, but rates may differ from those you
previously enjoyed through your employer's group plan. Before
deciding to go with an individual policy, ask yourself several questions:

- Is your health questionable? Life insurance may be a very important consideration.
- If you have your own life insurance policies, do you really need
  additional coverage? Do you need it now, or can it wait until you're
  reemployed?
- Even if you don't have other life insurance policies; if you are
  young, unmarried, or married to a working spouse; if you are
  without children or with grown children; or if you have no need
  to leave an estate, do you need this coverage now? Can it wait
  until you're reemployed?
- If some but not all of the foregoing applies to you (perhaps you're
  not so young, for example, but you're in good health), and you
  think you'll be employed again in the foreseeable future, could
  you do without the life insurance coverage for a reasonable time?
- If you're looking hard at reducing expenses over the short term,
  how difficult does an insurance broker think that it will be to
  obtain life insurance on your own (with proof of insurability, which
  may mean no more than a physical examination) some months
  hence when your financial situation may be clearer?

The answers to these questions will tell you whether obtaining life
insurance is a necessity or a luxury while you're out of work.

If you elect to purchase your own policy and your insurance is
held by a trust, check to ensure that the assignment is continuous.

## Long-Term Disability Insurance

Disability insurance has a universal application: It provides for replacement earnings in the event you are disabled through an illness,
accident, or injury and are unable to work. It's very likely you'll be
able to negotiate for extended disability coverage if you are ill or

injured at the time you are terminated, for the reasons discussed in chapter 7. As a rule, when you are unemployed, you won't be able to purchase disability insurance, because there's no stream of earnings to replace.

☞ Obtaining replacement long-term disability insurance is more critical if you don't plan on finding a new job but, instead, plan to be self-employed. Insurance companies will require a waiting period of up to a year following the start of a new business because the income stream is uncertain and the insurance company won't insure what doesn't exist.

The best strategy is to obtain disability insurance *before you are terminated.* If the termination comes as a surprise, get to an insurance broker quickly. In some instances the broker can position a separation package that continues for a significant time, such as a year or more, as a consulting contract. That helps clarify your earnings stream for at least the first period of self-employment. (Incidentally, if your new business is operating out of your home, you may need to add "business pursuits" to your homeowners policy. Check it out.)

## Other Insurance Tips

• When obtaining conversion insurance, opt for the *monthly* payment option since you always have the right to cancel at any time. This will allow you to move quickly to cancel unnecessary or duplicate expenses if you get a new job and are covered by your new employer's program.

• You are usually better off with an insurance broker who does business with a number of insurance companies rather than contacting an agent of an insurance company. If you don't know an insurance broker, ask your attorney or accountant for a recommendation. There's nothing wrong with doing business with someone's brother-in-law—provided you're aware that perhaps a family tie, as opposed to unadulterated professional admiration, has prompted the referral.

• Remember to check your beneficiaries when going through your personnel file. Negotiating vigorously with your employer for life insurance continuation, which prompts your untimely demise, and then having that money go to the wrong beneficiary would indeed be tragic.

A final grim thought: If your termination is prompted by a corporate reorganization that has led you to conclude your employer is no longer financially solvent, forget negotiating insurance continuation and find your own coverage. Fast.

## MAXIMIZING EMPLOYER-SPONSORED BENEFITS

Your employer has an obligation to provide you with information concerning your employer-sponsored benefits, including the balances you have in certain plans as well as employer and government restrictions and regulations. In general, your employer is obliged to communicate these details to you within sixty days of your termination date, if not sooner, depending on the nature of the benefit, and you have a limited time to respond with your decisions. It's a good idea to think these things through now, so you can act quickly when the time comes in order to keep your money working for you.

Six benefit plans are typically available to employees:

1. Pension plans
2. 401(k) plans (tax-deferred savings plans)
3. Stock purchase plans
4. Employee stock ownership plans (ESOPs)
5. Incentive stock options (ISOs) and stock appreciation rights (SARs)
6. Miscellaneous benefit plans that may be non(tax)qualified

### Pension Plans

A pension is a plan to which your employer makes contributions on your behalf and that provides for a specific benefit when you retire. In general, if your company provides such a plan, and you have worked there for more than five years, by law you are fully vested in that plan, meaning that you are entitled to receive that benefit. (There may be vesting exceptions in older plans, such as in collective bargaining or union plans.) If you've worked for your company for fewer than five years, you'll need to find out if there is partial vesting; for example, 20 percent per year for each of the five years. You are entitled—and encouraged—to request a summary plan description for this plan (as well as any others your employer provides). Check the vesting requirements to find out if you have any equity in the plan. Typically, you will receive an annual statement that will tell you your status.

*Payment Options.* Assuming that you are entitled to a benefit under your pension plan, the next step is to examine payment options. Most pension plans have a variety of payment options, including joint and survivor annuity, single life annuity, and period certain annuity. Some also provide for lump-sum payments. With a joint and survivor annuity, your plan makes a commitment to pay you at retirement age a specific monthly benefit; when you die, the plan will continue to pay your spouse a portion of the monthly payment previously provided to you. Such an annuity is known as a 50 percent joint and survivor annuity; 100 percent of the amount due goes to you while you are alive, and 50 percent goes to your spouse after your death.

You may choose a single life annuity to obtain a larger monthly payment, but once you die, the plan ceases payment altogether. If you are married, you must obtain your spouse's written, notarized permission to choose a single life payment option.

A period certain annuity payment is a promise to pay a benefit for a specified period, ten or twenty years, for example, to either you or your beneficiary. A lump sum is a complete payment made at one time without any further payments made in the future.

If the types of payments available to you are not listed here, don't be shy about asking for clear explanations. You shouldn't care if your company's pension department thinks you're a pain—it's *your money* we're discussing here. Best of all, you don't have to worry about this right now, unless you're over age fifty-five and are considering taking payments. If you are under age fifty-five, you're not eligible to receive these payments until you reach retirement age, which you can elect any time after you reach age fifty-five. Recognize, however, that your benefit, if taken prior to age sixty-five, will be *dramatically* reduced. While pension formulas vary, if you receive your pension benefit at age fifty-five, expect it to be reduced by about two-thirds; at age sixty, by about one third. That's because the actuarial assumption is that you'll be receiving these benefits over a longer period. If poor health is an issue, factor that into the equation, too. If you're close to age fifty-five, you should consult a financial adviser to determine the right option for you and your family. If not, you don't have to decide today at what age you want the benefit.

If your plan has a lump-sum option, it's almost always better to take the lump sum and invest it with the help of a qualified financial adviser. You will probably do a much better job of growing these dollars than your very conservative pension plan investment committee has (they're not incompetent; they just don't want to get sued). This decision, however, does depend on your cash flow needs, your health, and the health of your spouse if you have one, so get a professional to crunch the numbers.

☞ Most accountants and financial planners can help you figure out what's best for you, as can some brokers and insurance agents, usually for a small fee and sometimes on a complimentary basis.

If you take a lump sum, there are a number of things you should know, which are described in detail in the 401(k) plan section that follows.

Regardless of how you take your pension benefit, it's important that you recognize that this benefit is not intended by your employer to provide you with a *fully funded* retirement. Rather, it is intended to supplement your own savings and investments, as well as any government benefits that may exist at the time you retire, such as Social Security. The more money you make, the less significant the impact of a pension benefit will be on your lifestyle, since the government limits the amount of income that can be reflected in your company's contributions to high-wage earners.

*Pension Tips.*　　　Here are three final notes on pension plans:

• Assuming you are not taking your benefit now, it's your obligation to keep your former employer informed of your whereabouts. Whenever you move to a new residence, you must notify them, so they can contact you when you do reach retirement age or if anything happens to change the plan and/or its benefits. *It's not their obligation to find you. In this era of corporate change, you must continue to follow your former company in the news, making sure you are aware of mergers, acquisitions, name changes, headquarters relocations, and so on.*

•   Most companies do not allow anyone other than a spouse or minor child to be the beneficiary of your pension plan benefit. If you're not married and have no minor children, and you die prior to being eligible to receive your benefit, no one gets it—or, rather, your former employer gets to keep the money. Times—and corporate policies—are changing, however; if you are unmarried, it's a good idea to check on your former employer's policy periodically to determine if the policy at your company has changed, allowing you to name a beneficiary other than a minor child or spouse.

•   Finally, and this applies to all company benefits, the laws governing such plans change. Your company will likely notify you if anything significant changes.

### 401(k) Plans (Tax-Deferred Savings Plans)

Over the last fifteen years, many employers have turned to the 401(k) plan as an alternative to the traditional pension plan. The 401(k) plan is a defined contribution plan, a retirement vehicle that is funded largely, if not entirely, by you. If you are a teacher or other public employee, you may have a similar plan known as a 403(b) plan; it operates pretty much the same as the 401(k). Here's how such plans work when you leave your employer:

Within sixty days of your termination, you will receive a package outlining your plan balances. This will also provide you with instructions on how to proceed and will describe the decisions you'll have to make. In general, you'll have three choices, and *these will not wait until you reach an eligible retirement age*:

1.   Leave the money in your company-sponsored plan.
2.   Roll the money over into the plan of your new employer, *or*
3.   Take the money and put it in an IRA *Rollover* account.

☞   You do have a fourth choice, which is to simply take direct receipt of the funds, but if you are under age fifty-nine and a half, you will be subject to a 10 percent penalty in addition to substantial taxation. If you do not need your 401(k) money to make ends meet during your unemployment, don't take direct receipt of it. These funds should only be used as a last resort, since they are growing tax deferred. (Your *after-tax* contributions to your 401(k) can be paid out to you without incurring a penalty tax. But we still believe you should regard this as money of last resort.)

To make matters worse, any check made out directly to you will be subject to a 20 percent withholding tax. If you decide, fifty-eight days later, that you don't need the money after all, you will have to deposit the proceeds received from your employer, *along with the 20 percent your employer withheld*. Since your employer has already forwarded that money to the government, you'll have to come up with the 20 percent on your own, which could be a significant burden to you even if you've found a new job.

While, once again, you should consult your financial adviser, it's almost always advisable to take receipt of your plan balance in a check or stock shares if applicable (not made out to you!) and roll it over to an IRA. Employer-sponsored plans, whether at your current or future employer, are generally limited to perhaps as few as three or as many as eight to ten investment alternatives. With an IRA rollover, you will have many more investment alternatives available to you. And once you're reemployed, if your new employer's plan is better than your IRA, you can take your IRA rollover money and deposit it into your new employer's 401(k). (The benefit to redepositing your money into a 401(k) is that many employers' 401(k) plans permit loans, whereas you can't make a loan to yourself from an IRA account.)

Prior to responding to your company's request for instructions, if you intend to roll over your plan balance to an IRA, you must open an IRA rollover account. You can open such an account at any brokerage firm, as well as most banks and mutual fund companies. When you have obtained the account number, provide it to your employer with instructions to make the check payable to that institution *as IRA Custodian*. The form you receive from your employer should provide you with the space and instructions to do so.

In this way, the check that will be deposited in your account will *not* be subject to the required 20 percent withholding tax. As a point of information, an IRA rollover has the same benefits as an IRA; your assets will grow tax deferred.

## Stock Purchase Plans

Many publicly traded companies provide their employees with the opportunity to purchase stock on a regular basis through payroll deduction. More often than not, these plans provide the additional benefit of buying the stock at a discount. It's a great way to accumulate savings, but if you liquidate the shares, you may be subject to ordinary income tax on the portion of the proceeds derived from the benefit of the discount, depending on how long you have held the stock. In other words, if you bought the stock at $10.00 per share with a 15 percent discount, paying $8.50 per share, and you sell the stock at $12.00, the $2.00 profit is subject to capital gains tax, generally at a lower rate, but the $1.50 profit arising from the discount will be subject to ordinary income tax.

Most plans have a two- or three-year holding period on shares. Check your summary plan description and consult a tax or financial adviser on how you should handle receipt of your shares. You have the option of taking the shares, rather than liquidating them and taking cash, but prior to making the decision, you should talk to your investment adviser about your diversification needs.

## Employee Stock Ownership Plans (ESOPs)

An employee stock ownership plan is a profit-sharing plan, except that your company's contribution to the plan on your behalf is in the form of shares of the company's stock. An ESOP differs from a stock purchase plan because your company contributes the shares of stock in an ESOP rather than you buying them. Upon termination, your ESOP balance is treated in the same manner as your 401(k) or other tax-deferred savings plan. Again, as with your 401(k), think through the tax implications carefully.

## Incentive Stock Options (ISOs) and Stock Appreciation Rights (SARs)

You may have received incentive stock options (ISOs) or stock appreciation rights (SARs) from your employer during the course of your employment. Once you have been terminated, you will have a limited time in which to exercise any vested options or rights you may been awarded, often between thirty days and six months, depending on your employer's policy. Explicit restrictions apply to directors, owners, and anyone with availability to insider information, and you may need to consult a tax adviser about your rights and obligations. If your vested options or rights are "in the money," meaning that the price at which you can buy the stock through the plan is lower than the price at which it's currently trading, you should exercise your options.

Usually, your company will supply you with a form to request the exercise; if it doesn't, ask for it. When you exercise, you are buying the stock at the specified, or "strike," price. That means that you will have to provide the cash to buy the stock. Since you will be making a profit, you will also have to pay the income taxes on that profit. Because the difference between the price you paid and the price of the stock is considered compensation, it is taxed as ordinary income, rather than as a capital gain.

If you already own stock through a stock purchase plan or are vested in the stock of your company in the form of restricted stock that you must hold, consider selling stock acquired through the exercise of options in order to gain more diversification. Again, consult your financial adviser. If you exercise your "in the money" options or rights and sell in one transaction, you must still pay the tax, but you will gain the proceeds from the sale upon settlement of the transaction. Many employers, and almost all brokerage firms, will perform a "cashless" exercise for you, enabling you to acquire the stock and sell it without putting up the money to acquire it. You only have to provide the money to cover your taxes, because the money to acquire the stock is made available by selling off the requisite number of shares.

## Other Benefit Plans

Some employers offer an array of plans not discussed here. These are known as nonqualified plans, meaning that not all employees are eligible for them and therefore these plans don't qualify for certain tax benefits. These may include deferred compensation plans and restricted stock award programs that are subject to restrictions established by your employer, which may vary significantly from employer to employer.

Since you may not be eligible to reap benefits from nonqualified plans for some time following your departure from the company, the same rules that apply to your pension plan apply here. For example, some restricted stock plans become immediately unrestricted and fully vested in the event of a merger or acquisition. Let your former employer know where you are, and keep tabs on the news regarding your employer.

When you're employed, reading about your benefit plans can be very confusing or downright boring. Human resources people and attorneys have made an art of writing unintelligible language for employees to decipher. When you're separating from your company, it be even more daunting. Dealing with these issues, together with the trauma of leaving your employer, the stress of finding a new job, and making ends meet, can be extremely difficult. While procrastination may be, as the poet says, the thief of time, in this case it may well be the thief of your financial well-being. Don't delay, and don't try to figure it out for yourself. Get advice from people with the expertise to help.

# 13

# DON'T HIDE IT UNDER YOUR MATTRESS

If you've concluded your separation negotiations by putting into practice the strategies we've recommended—as well as following the dictates of your own good sense—then you've probably improved your financial package. Your separation check, combined with your cash and savings, represents significant money. How significant it is will be determined by your current status. If you've strolled from the rear door of your former job through the front door of your next, you'll treat your separation money one way. If you've trudged out of your last job into the empty streets of unemployment, you'll be forced to treat your separation money another way. In either case, plan on investing it. And by "investing" we do not mean putting your money into any of the following (just in case you've been tempted):

- That terrifically sexy sports car
- The chance to double your money instantly at the blackjack table
- The opportunity to back the inventions of an old friend who you know could succeed if she'd only been given half a chance
- The world cruise of a lifetime in your own yacht that just happens to measure twice the length of your former boss's dinghy

And so on. (You get the picture.)

In any event, this is a crucial time to examine your investment options in either of the two situations you may now find yourself. Consider either:

- How to invest if you're unemployed, *or*
- How to invest if you're employed

196

## HOW TO INVEST IF YOU'RE UNEMPLOYED

If you're unemployed, you should have two objectives when it comes to managing cash: first, *to conserve it*, and second, *to stretch it*. Neither will be accomplished by depositing this money in a non–interest-bearing checking account or in an intelligence-insulting savings account paying minimal interest. What do you do?

☞ *Immediately* deposit your cash—all of it—into an interest-bearing money-market fund offered by banks or brokerage firms. A money-market fund is a mutual fund that invests in very short-term fixed-income securities. While it's not completely risk free, no one has ever failed to get back the face amount of an investment.

With a money-market fund, you can be confident that your principal will be safe while you earn a reasonable rate of interest. There are two types of money-market funds: taxable and tax-exempt. If, because you are unemployed, your new combined tax rate is 35 percent or higher, choose a tax-exempt fund. If you're subject to high state and city taxes, your combined rate is likely to be above 35 percent. Most fund companies offer individual state triple tax-exempt funds, particularly for such high-tax states as New York, New Jersey, Massachusetts, California, Connecticut, and a handful of others.

☞ *A cautionary note*: Be aware of money-market-fund account-opening fees, annual charges, or minimum-balance requirements. Don't pay out more in costs than you can earn in interest.

***Cash Flow Revisited.***   It's important to understand your cash flow needs—that is, how much money will you need per month to pay your bills and how many months will you have the money to pay them? In chapter 4 you developed a budget to help calculate your separation pay needs. Retrieve that final worksheet to help manage your cash. Take the figure at the bottom of the worksheet— your total monthly expenses—and divide it into the total amount of cash on hand. The result will be the number of months you can live off your cash on hand. Here's an example: Let's say that you need $3,000 per month after taxes to live, and that you have $35,000 in cash. $35,000 divided by $3,000 equals 11.7 months. That means that you can pay your bills for almost a year. Add to this the interest you'll earn on the balance still in the money-market fund, as well as the weeks of unemployment benefits you'll receive, and you've stretched your cash past the twelve-month mark. In any event, this information should help decide your choice of investment vehicles and how much attention you'll need to pay to tax considerations in choosing your investments.

***Tax Considerations.***   On a purely cash flow basis, taxable investments always pay more interest than tax-exempt investments. So if you don't have a lot of money or a lot of time, you'll want to maximize your yield (within acceptable parameters of safety) and worry about the taxes later when you have a job. The incremental interest you earn will probably cover you only during another week or two of unemployment, but in your situation every little bit will help. Consult the business pages of your Sunday newspaper. Most carry current rates for the highest-yielding money funds. Find the highest-yielding taxable money fund you can, and deposit your cash on hand.

## HOW TO INVEST IF YOU'RE EMPLOYED

You came out a winner! You were terminated, you negotiated a good separation package, and you quickly found another job. Therefore, your separation package won't have to be used to keep the wolf from the door. You have *SAVINGS*, and you have flexibility in terms of your investments.

But before getting into actual investments and investment strategies, let's examine some basics. You want to have some of your money in each of three major categories: cash, equity, and income investments.

• *Cash/cash equivalents.* Investments classified as cash are characterized by their *high liquidity* and *low risk* to the safety of your principal.

- *Equity/growth.* Investments classified as equity investments (ideally) *appreciate* in value.
- *Income.* Investments classified as income *produce a steady stream of income* for the investor.

**Cash/Cash Equivalents.**   Cash or cash equivalents are characterized by the safety afforded to your principal, through investments such as a bank deposit, money-market fund, or a short-term certificate of deposit. Your allocation to cash must include the traditional cash reserve, at the very least. The financial planner's rule of thumb is a minimum of three months' to a maximum of six months' expenses. A more conservative rule is six to twelve months. If your other investments are liquid, three to six months' reserve should be enough.

**Equity/growth.**   Equity or growth investments are made in real estate or a listed or unlisted security (stock). These investments are characterized by providing higher overall returns over a long period while being subject to greater fluctuation over the short term.

Here are four broad rules of thumb about equity investments:

1. The longer your time horizon or the younger you are, the more you should put in equity investments.
2. The higher your tolerance for market risk, the more you should put into equity investments.
3. The lower your tolerance for inflation risk, the more you should put into equity investments.
4. The lower your needs for income, the more you should put into equity investments.

There are no absolutes when it comes to asset allocation, but one well-regarded investment strategist never puts more than 70 percent into equity and never less than 5 percent into cash. Tax considerations play a large role in equity investments as well.

*Income.* Income investments produce a steady stream of income for the investor, such as five-year bank certificates of deposit or bonds. If you need (as opposed to *want*) current income, invest in securities so that you'll have it. How much you invest depends upon how much income you need. For example, if you require $5,000 per year in pretax income from your investments, you would need to invest $50,000 at 10 percent to obtain that level of income, or $100,000 at 5 percent.

Fixed-income investments provide two methods of achieving higher returns—*security* and *maturity* selection. The higher your tolerance for credit risk, the more aggressive your security selection can be. Credit risk pertains to the issuer's ability to meet its obligations. This concept is very similar to a bank issuing you a credit card or a loan. The bank evaluates your ability to pay the debt back, and assumes the credit risk of lending you money.

Maturity selection is equally critical. If you can afford to wait for your principal while receiving income, you can generally achieve higher rates of return by investing for longer periods. The shorter your time horizon, as long as it's in excess of a year or so, the more you should put into income investments rather than in equity. Most people believe stocks are among the riskiest investments. That's true, if your time horizon for investing is just a year or two. Over time, more of the risks are removed from investing in any type of investment vehicle, including stocks.

Keep in mind that equities do a better job of outperforming inflation than traditional fixed-income vehicles. If inflation ever returns to historic highs, it will erode your buying power. For example, if inflation is moving at a rate of 3 percent, you have to earn at least that much on your cash to maintain your purchasing power and your standard of living.

Finally, some investments are hybrids—for example, real estate. Investors may own real estate that can produce rental income and may also appreciate in value. Examples of other hybrids include stocks that pay a substantial dividend, and convertible bonds that pay interest like a bond but participate in the growth of the underlying equity.

With the multiplicity of different types of risk out there, it's a miracle that people even bother to invest. But they do. Why not consider the alternative and leave your money in your mattress? That too is risky. Aside from the danger of theft or fire, you'll be guaranteed to miss every opportunity to increase your savings.

# CHOOSING THE BEST INVESTMENT DISTRIBUTION FOR YOU

How much should you invest in each of these categories? That depends on your tolerance for the different types of risks involved, your time horizon, your tax situation, and the purpose of the funds you're investing. Use the Investment Questionnaire to examine your circumstances.

Filling out the questionnaire is not a substitute for consulting a competent investment adviser, such as a lawyer, financial planner, accountant, stockbroker, or private banker. Our objective is to point you in the right direction; your objective is to control your finances by getting the advice you need. Find someone whose track history can be verified and whose advice feels comfortable.

Now take some of your hard-earned separation pay and make it work even harder for you. You've already lived with the risk of unemployment; these other risks are tame by comparison.

---

### Investment Questionnaire

*Source*: N-Compass Financial Services, Ltd., c/o Tremont Advisers, Inc., Rye, New York

1. **What is your age?**
   (1) 18–25
   (2) 26–40
   (3) 41–55
   (4) 56–65
   (5) Over 65

2. **What is the expected time horizon of your portfolio?**
   (1) I expect to require use of my assets within three years.
   (2) I expect to require use of my assets within three to seven years.
   (3) I do not expect to require use of my assets for seven years or more.

3. **What is your current income requirement from this portfolio?**
   (1) I am dependent on income for my lifestyle.

(2) I need a portion of income for my lifestyle.

(3) I do not require current income.

4. **What is the primary objective for your investments in this program?**

   (1) *Income/preservation of capital.* The safety of my money is my primary objective. I would rather have a low, but fixed rate of return than jeopardize any portion of my principal.

   (2) *Income and growth.* I am seeking to emphasize current income, but would like the opportunity for moderate capital growth.

   (3) *Growth and income.* I am seeking to emphasize capital growth but would like a moderate level of current income.

   (4) *Capital appreciation.* I am seeking to maximize capital appreciation and do not require current income.

5. **What best describes your tolerance for risk or changes in the value of your portfolio?**

   (1) *Conservative.* I am uncomfortable with price volatility and am willing to give up higher returns in order to keep most of my principal intact.

   (2) *Conservative/moderate.* I expect the value of my investment to fluctuate, but not drastically.

   (3) *Moderate.* I am willing to accept moderate fluctuations in the value of my investment, which should allow me to achieve modest growth.

   (4) *Moderate/aggressive.* I am seeking the greatest potential for capital growth and realize that there may be significant and prolonged declines in the value of my portfolio.

   (5) *Aggressive.* I am seeking the greatest potential for capital growth. I can tolerate more than one year of negative returns through difficult phases in the market and am willing to assume a high degree of risk.

6. **On a scale of 1 to 5, rank your risk tolerance, with 1 being very income/capital preservation–oriented and 5 being focused on aggressive growth and tolerant of greater volatility in exchange for the possibility of achieving much higher than average returns.**

## Scoring Key

*Add up your points*

### For question 1, if you answered:

(1) Add 1 point
(2) Add 2 points
(3) Add 3 points
(4) Add 4 points
(5) Add 5 points

### For question 2, if you answered:

(1) Add 1 point
(2) Add 3 points
(3) Add 5 points

### For question 3, if you answered:

(1) Add 1 point
(2) Add 3 points
(3) Add 5 points

### For question 4, if you answered:

(1) Add 1 point
(2) Add 2 points
(3) Add 4 points
(4) Add 5 points

### For question 5, if you answered:

(1) Add 1 point
(2) Add 2 points
(3) Add 3 points
(4) Add 4 points
(5) Add 5 points

### For question 6, if you answered:

(1) Add 1 point
(2) Add 2 points
(3) Add 3 points
(4) Add 4 points
(5) Add 5 points

**You can have a low of 6 points or a high of 30. Here's what your score means:**

• If you scored between 6 and 12 points, chances are you do not skydive for relaxation and would not be comfortable as a serious equity investor. You should conduct your investing activities in a manner that exposes your portfolio to little or no risk.

• If you scored between 13 and 21 points, you are a moderate investor. You should strive for a balance between equity and intermediate-term fixed-income investments that is adjusted by your age. At thirty-five, for example, you might want to have 60 percent of your money in conservative equities and 40 percent in fixed-income instruments. By the time you reach age fifty-five, you would likely switch that mix to put 60 percent of your investment into fixed income and 40 percent in equities. And you'd only skydive on a bet that had a *big* payoff.

• If you scored between 22 and 30 points, you are a bet-the-ranch investor. You are therefore willing to take relatively high degrees of risk in an effort to obtain higher-than-average returns. A substantial percentage of your portfolio needs to be in equity-type investments. Consider investing 10 percent, 15 percent, or 20 percent of your portfolio in areas that are high risk (small cap, technology, or emerging markets) so that you can get the kind of opportunity for return that would not be otherwise available in a lower-risk category. And remember your parachute.

# 14

# TAKING CONTROL OF
# YOUR FUTURE

If you've recently gone through the travail of negotiating a satisfactory severance package for yourself, you were able to solve some gritty problems—problems that you may once have thought insoluble. If you're feeling relief now that the thing's finally done, don't let your guard down yet. You'll soon deal with the familiar issues of control and accountability again—not necessarily because you'll be terminated, but because these issues will continue to affect *every* aspect of your employment. Terminations and layoffs have become a mainstay in the American economy. They're routine management tools used in bad times and good, and it's easier to cope with the possibility of a termination that you've considered early on— such as at your time of *hire*. This kind of thinking is crucial in setting up new employment on terms you can live with. How well you set this up will depend on your answers to two questions: What have you learned from your recent research, termination, and negotiations? How will what you've learned help you in your life, as well as in your next job?

One thing you probably learned is that you can no longer depend on the parental protection of an employer to take care of financial and other essentials you might previously have regarded as "not my responsibility." You should have concluded that only by taking on the full burden of your own welfare in the workplace can you create a measure of security for yourself and your family. Taking responsibility means keeping your eyes open, planning, and as you did in your separation negotiations, strategizing.

# TAKING RESPONSIBILITY

How can you take the responsibility for your security—emotional as well as financial—from your employer's hands and put it into your own? Here are several steps:

- Examine your past beliefs about work.
- Learn to think like an entrepreneur.
- Review lessons learned from your recent past—your termination and everything that led up to it—for clues about how you can prosper in an era of job insecurity.

## Examine Your Past Beliefs about Work

Our culture offers us a great range of attitudes about work, including those that soar to the lofty (*Work is something made greater by ourselves and in turn that makes us greater.*—Maya Angelou), down through the desperate (*Work is life, you know, and without it, there's nothing but fear and insecurity.*—John Lennon), and further, to the comically contemptible (*Work is the curse of the drinking classes.*—Oscar Wilde).

Some attitudes that may have had validity in the past are no longer helpful. In fact, they are a hindrance to us, and should be reviewed closely. Let's examine the three myths of corporate life:

1. The company will take care of me.
2. My co-workers are my extended family.
3. I am my job.

*1. The company will take care of me.*   Despite galloping corporate profits, jobs that in the past seemed essential and stable are being eliminated. A typical employee, working into the next century, should be prepared to pledge allegiance to at least eight or more employers during his or her work life. Old-fashioned company loyalty—which means both the loyalty of workers to their jobs and the loyalty of the company to its workers—is almost a dead issue, something the highest-flying CEO and the lowest, most vulnerable worker now agree on.

Was there really a golden age when employees worked for one

company all their lives, and the company, for its part, took care of all the workers' needs? In truth, and with few and particular exceptions (and these, for limited periods), there never was such a time of employer-employee partnership, at least not since the beginnings of the Industrial Revolution after the Civil War. Had these benevolent working conditions existed as the rule and not the exception, we would not have seen the rise of the labor union movement and the necessity of child labor laws in this country, nor the socialist and communist worker's revolutions in Europe and elsewhere.

Companies always need to profit, and their employees are the agents and tools for that. And while many large companies in the past attempted to provide their workers with long-term job security, that endeavor is ending. Companies are responding to changing times by changing the rules by which they deal with workers. How much job security any company will be willing to guarantee its employees is an open question, now and in the foreseeable future.

**2. *My co-workers are my extended family.***     If you were able to see your termination coming by the danger signals we discussed in chapter 1, you may already be convinced that your co-workers, likable and helpful souls as they may have been during good times, are not really part of your protective, extended family. When the bad times came, many of them disappointed you. Either they weren't there for you or they weren't able to solve your problems. If they felt threatened themselves, they were running for cover. Even if they thought they were safe, they were probably showing you a side of themselves you hadn't seen before: a cold, distant, suspicious, or cruel side. But what made you think you were all part of a great big family?

Two things. First, it's natural to make friends with co-workers. After all, you spend a great part of your life with them, and it's important for everyone's peace of mind to get along. Second, it's in the company's interests that employees *bond to something or to somebody*—despite all the talk of a new, noncommittal social contract in the workplace. A company without a shared sense of community, in which workers regularly lie, cheat, and steal from each other, and pass on proprietary information to competitors for quick cash, is a company that's not long for this world.

Companies have made attempts over the years (sometimes by hit-or-miss; sometimes by design) to foster loyalty among workers. The usual incentives, such as salary increases, bonuses, perks, paid insurance, retirement benefits, and so on, have been supplemented by training programs. Most recently, one pervasive fad, marketed under a variety of brand names, has had great success fostering the illusion of the extended family at work. It consists of programs that emphasize teamwork—especially each member's loyalty to others on the team. These programs are expensive to implement (although not nearly as expensive as giving workers real guarantees of job security), and they gobble up precious time in each member's daily routine. The real problem with these colorful butterflies of idealistic inspiration, though, is when push comes to shove, they fall to the floor, useless as ill-designed paper airplanes.

---

### Notes from the Firing Line

*In the absence of workplace guarantees, companies have invested in programs to artificially promote employee loyalty. Most of these fall flat on their faces:*

Some time ago I took a freelance job with a large television production company. My assignment was to join a group of writers at work on a short-term project seriously behind schedule. Despite the urgency of our mission, each workday was interrupted by meetings, some lasting over two hours. The purpose of these was to develop corporate team spirit as an antidote to some recent firings and defections. We were drilled in the Seven Commandments of Team Spirit, which begin with the declaration that all members are equal—supervisors and fellow toilers alike—and end with the solemn vow to protect our co-workers above everything else.

Despite their length, these meetings exposed us to some strategies that had they been given a chance, might have done some good in our office. A few weeks before the completion of the project, an order from management that my department again be downsized created a panic. Supervisors and employees at all levels began a cutthroat scramble for survival. The Seven Commandments of Team Spirit were abandoned when they might have done the most good. The only positive result I could see in all this was the temporary end to team meetings. This allowed those of us remaining to finish our project with relative efficiency.

—Alexander, writer, age 48

A program to raise the spiritual values of the workplace stands no chance within a fragmented corporate culture that fails to take spiritual values seriously. Aside from being colossal time-wasters, these programs further the illusion that the workplace is an extended family. It isn't.

**3. *I am my job.*** What often hurts more than the act of leaving a job is the emptiness that can overtake you after the initial shock has faded.

---

### Notes from the Firing Line

*If you've overly identified yourself with your job, you'll be left without an anchor when you leave your work:*

I was the manager of a clothing factory for thirty years. Until the last couple of years, I'd really enjoyed my work. It was never dull: one minute I'd be setting up the new patterns; the next, I'd be hiring and firing. We had some great years, and I did very well. But then my boss at work started going crazy. He contracted to manufacture some very complex dresses. We began putting in long hours and weekends, but our equipment wasn't up to the work. We'd struggle to get one order done, and before we knew it, the one we'd shipped a week before would be returned because it had too many defective pieces. My boss spent all day yelling and screaming at me to get the women to work harder, and he wouldn't listen when I told him we were doing our best. These new orders were killing us. Finally, I had to quit. I've been gone from there two years, and I'm glad I got out. These days, mostly, I take walks. I don't know what to do with myself. Sometimes I drive down to the factory and look at the building from down the block. I keep thinking, even though it was awful there at the end, at least I knew what I was doing. Unlike now.

—Tim, manager, age 56

---

This emptiness can be explained in one sentence: *I define myself through my job.* It results from specialization and longstanding, narrow-banded, habitual behavior. When you have your work, you feel like somebody. Not necessarily SOMEBODY, in the overinflated sense, but a person, comfortably defined. On the flip side, without your job, you feel like nobody—a meaningless entity, drifting end-lessly through the long day. During the first couple of weeks after you leave your job, you might treat yourself to long-denied luxuries, such as leisurely antique shopping, a fishing trip, or going to the movies during the afternoon. But against your expectations, the antiques are dusty and overpriced; you discover you don't really care for fish, anyway; and the low-priced matinee movie rates are fine, but after a few days, you're sick of popcorn. You find yourself rambling around, feeling guilty. You look up at the office building in front of you and wonder what it would be like to work there. This life of leisure isn't as great as it was cracked up to be, you conclude. Meanwhile, in all the office windows, people are looking down at you, thinking, "*Wow. I wish I could rip off this suit and go watch a movie like whoever that is down there!*"

Your unease isn't helped when you meet people socially, and the first question you're likely to be asked is "What do you do?" Perhaps now you better understand the plight of homemakers who respond to that question defensively, explaining that they work their brains out every day, but not in an office building. This is when you long for the 1960s when people seemed more interested in knowing your astro-logical sign.

Ideally, your termination will have been liberating in this respect: You're not just what you do for a living. You are a host of intercon-nected hopes, dreams, fears, and complex thoughts. No two people view you as the same—to one you might be someone's neighbor with the stupid dog; to another, you're a big-tipping coffee purchaser; to another, an uncool, tyrannical parent; and on and on. None of these people see you as only one thing—a wage earner—so why should you take such a limited view of yourself? If you cede the power to your former employer to wipe out your identity with the stroke of a pen on a separation agreement, you're giving up too much. They can do it again tomorrow—to you or the guy in the office across the hall. Do you really want to hinge your existence to such extraneous events?

## Learn to Think Like an Entrepreneur

The employer-employee relationship has always been a kind of devil's bargain in which the employer offers financial and social comfort in return for your soul. In this case, your soul consists of a good amount of your autonomy and personal responsibility. As comfortable and equitable as this bargain once was, it has become a one-sided affair, since employers are increasingly unwilling to fulfill their part of it. But what is the solution? You'll still have to work. How can the deal be made sweeter on your side? Having lost a job, you're now in a great position to think this through, as you prepare for your next one.

☞ *More than anything, this book has been about taking control.* By "control," we mean taking responsibility for yourself. The things you formerly left to the care of your employer are a good starting place. In approaching your next job, you should not docilely agree to the functions and benefits offered to you. Be prepared to negotiate every step of the way until you've crafted an understanding each party can live with—and prosper. To do this, you'll have to stop thinking like an employee and start thinking like an entrepreneur.

If you've worked for a company all your life, your goal now may be to find a workplace identical to the one you've left behind. Increasingly, people leaving the corporate environment are opting to begin their own businesses, or to become partners with others in smaller settings. You may never have thought of yourself as an entrepreneur; you may not even find the idea interesting. But now, as you're planning your next career move, take a look at the table on page 212, which compares some simple aspects of the life of an employee of a corporation to that of an entrepreneur.

Who has the better life, the employee or the entrepreneur? Obviously, the answer depends on who you are. Are you an employee, happy to exchange much of your freedom to chose where, when, and with whom you work for an employer's promise to provide a regular paycheck and some benefits? Or are you an entrepreneur, willing to undergo the rigors and privations of bad economic years for the rewards of good ones? No matter how you answer, the point is, employees cede control and get back only what's offered them in return. Entrepreneurs, on the other hand, take risks, stay on top of things, do all it takes to be successful, but at the end of the day, they're the ones who take home the winnings.

How can you start thinking more like an entrepreneur who's in control, and less like an employee without a clue? The first step is to

| Aspects for Control | Employee | Entrepreneur |
| --- | --- | --- |
| Work schedule | Decided by the company | Decided by you or the job you've contracted to perform |
| Work environment | Decided by the company | Wherever you can afford to have your office—could be at home, working in your pajamas |
| Health insurance | Decided by the company | Must find your own |
| Compensation | Decided by the company | Usually tied to profits |
| Vacations | Decided by the company | Whenever and wherever you wish or can afford |
| Perks | Decided by the company | No perks, or everything is a perk, depending on your point of view |
| Profits | Good to know about, but you may not see many of them coming your way | You keep them all |
| Losses | Unless they're severe, not usually your problem | You eat them all |

review how you got to where you are now, and what you learned from the journey.

## Review Lessons Learned from Your Recent Past

Once you're in your new job, your objective should be to remain there on the terms you and your employer agreed to when you accepted the job offer. But how can you monitor your day-to-day status within your new company in order to remain in control of your situation?

The answer is to apply the principles you learned from this book as you negotiated your way through your termination and separation from your former employer. Let's review them:

- Ask for what you really want, whether you think you'll get it or not.
- Be plugged in to what's going on around you.
- Keep your proverbial ducks in a row—monitor your position within the company.
- When you're told something important, give yourself time to think. Listen before you talk.
- Negotiate for everything in life.
- Recognize problems if they exist, and obtain professional help.

***Ask for what you really want, whether you think you'll get it or not.*** After you receive the right job offer from your next employer, enthusiastically accept it. Then tell your new employer that you'd like an employment contract that outlines what will happen in the event that you or the job doesn't work out. The contract should cover an enhanced severance package (since the formula under most written severance policies is meager in the absence of significant tenure), benefits continuation, bonus payments, and so forth. (You are now familiar with the drill.)

Your employer will likely refuse because an employment contract traditionally guarantees a *period* of employment. Unless you are supremely valuable to them, they'll want you to remain employed at their pleasure, allowing them to terminate you at any time, for any reason. Propose the following as a counteroffer: Ask for a letter that outlines your exit strategy. Say that one of the most important things that you've learned about business is that in any venture, an exit strategy is crucial. You'll always want to be prepared to cut your losses and get on with the next project. Explain that your termination package—in the *extremely* unlikely event (chuckle!) that the job doesn't work out—is important to you. If you're asked whether this means you don't believe you're the right person for the job, say confidently, *"I'm exactly the person you want working here; I hope for the best and plan for the worst."*

Then ask for a sign-on bonus or a performance bonus, relocation dollars if appropriate, an accelerated review on your salary increase, and early participation in benefit programs that might otherwise have a waiting period.

☞ What you shouldn't mention to your new employer at this juncture is that he or she can anticipate this negotiating behavior from you at periodic intervals—such as when you're thinking of transferring, accepting a promotion or reassignment, retiring, or departing. Negotiating is now part of your repertoire.

***Be plugged in to what's going on around you.***    As you did to determine your probable fate in your last job, keep your eyes and ears open for signs of significant things happening in your world. These signs include changes in the behavior of your co-workers, subordinates, and boss; changes in your assignments and responsibilities; changes in your perks; changes in company management; and changes in the company's financial position.

Along with listening to everything comes a caution that you should keep your own counsel. You may gather plenty of information, but do not become the fount of company gossip. Be discreet. No one respects or trusts someone with loose lips.

---

### Notes from the Firing Line

*Discretion is not only a moral virtue, it's practical as well:*

Everyone knew that Bob was in-the-know. He always seemed to be one step ahead of whatever unguided missile was hurtling toward the rest of us. And the reason we all knew this was, periodically, about ten minutes before everyone else learned about it, Bob would take you aside and tell you some incredible piece of information. There was never enough time for you to tell anyone else, so Bob never got the reputation for being indiscreet, but there was just enough time to persuade you Bob was really connected to the people and things that mattered. When I asked him for his secret, he told me that he just knew when and where to listen—and when and to whom to talk.

—Michael, packaging sales, age 50

In stressful situations, your intuition, informed by experience, can be your guide to the truth of things. If you feel as if control has suddenly been wrenched from you, then objectively analyze your feelings and suspicions. Are they based on real events? If so, find out what's behind them. Review chapter 1 if you're fuzzy on the details of how to go about this.

***Keep your proverbial ducks in a row—monitor your position within the company.***    The start of a new job will demand your concentration, but you should now establish crucial information resources you'll use to periodically monitor your situation. These resources fall into two categories: things and people.

Make a habit of inspecting your personnel file. Not much will be placed in this file by your employer unless you've gotten into some kind of trouble—or someone wants it to appear that way.

The first time you ask to see your file, read over any information supplied by your last employer—your criminal/credit check can be an unpleasant revelation. If necessary, take immediate action to correct misstatements, undocumented opinions, gratuitous comments, or outright lies. Review and retain the company's employee handbook and any summary plan descriptions. It's always useful to know what the company considers its minimal positions on employment rules and separation offers.

Make friends with someone in the human resources department and with others who know the company's past practices. Not only will you get a better understanding of the historical (that is, real) company practices, but you'll also have a friend who might act as a barometer or early warning system in the event things begin to go wrong for you.

Above all, when asking for information, or if you've made an unpleasant discovery in one of your files, always act in a friendly, businesslike manner. By doing this research, you are certainly within your rights, but you'll need the goodwill from those you depend on for answers. Smile and be confident: You're heading off trouble before it starts. Review chapter 2 for the specifics.

***When you're told something important, give yourself time to think. Listen before you talk.***    This lesson applies to just about everything in life. Does it make you faintly ill when people remind you about listening by saying, "There's a reason you have two ears but only one mouth." Get over your nausea. If you were the kid in grade school who got all the praise by waving your hand wildly in the air and yelling, *"I know the answer; I know the answer,"* recognize that there's more at stake today. Slow the action down around you, and give yourself time to think and plan. You're not a slow learner; you're thoughtful.

No matter what change of your status is being proposed—or announced as a done deed—control yourself. Whether you like what was proposed, you'll need time to think it over. Even small changes that seem to be harmless erosions or shifts of your authority need careful consideration. Instead, listen carefully to everything said. Do not immediately agree to anything. Do not debate your job performance, if that was in question. Do not make threats, especially threats to sue or go to the media. Do not start negotiations. And above all else, do not sign anything.

Instead, ask nonhostile questions to clarify points you don't understand or explore areas not addressed. Ask that propositions be made in writing. Set a date for your next meeting, giving you time to consider everything that was discussed. After the meeting concludes, make notes. Review chapter 3 for more specifics.

***Negotiate for everything in life.*** If you didn't consider yourself a negotiator before you put into action the techniques we've outlined for you in this book, you may look more favorably on the practice now. While money is often the root of many negotiations, two other areas can be successfully negotiated: nonmoney issues, such as persuading people to see and do things your way; and mixed issues, such as getting the job you want and, at the same time, negotiating salary. Most likely, the total compensation offered by your new employer includes more than just your pay. In addition, you have health care, vacation pay, retirement benefits, life insurance, stock/option packages, memberships, and so on. Each of these offers an opportunity for you to enhance your compensation by continually watching for the chance to renegotiate them. The key to being a successful negotiator is to analyze everything that's being offered to you—no matter how terrific—with an eye to seeing how it can be improved. Review chapter 9 for the methods.

***Recognize problems if they exist, and obtain professional help.*** It's natural to be upset and hurt by a termination, no matter the reasons for it. If you once assumed you were part of an extended family, supported and defended by the company for which you worked, your hurt at this rejection may be deep. As we've emphasized throughout this book, it would be a mistake for you to react to your dismissal by slamming the company door behind you. We've given you the strategy and the tools to craft the best departure package for yourself out of what is available, and we've counseled patience and courage on your part to make this happen. Another reason not to give in to the natural embarrassment of being fired has to do with your emotional health.

In chapter 2 we gave you the experience of Allen, a forty-seven-year-old distributor. You may recall that Allen had an affair with his assistant. After he broke off the relationship, his boss and the company attorney informed him that his assistant claimed Allen had raped her. Allen was speechless and dazed, and he offered no opposition to his termination. Only later, when he explained his circumstances to his friend, Allen acknowledged he had saved love letters his assistant had written to him before the breakup. Why, demanded his friend, had Allen not brought those letters to his boss, letters that would certainly have exonerated him? Allen's response was that it was all too embarrassing. He had preferred to leave quickly, so his reputation would not be damaged, his shame not known. The irony is that despite Allen's desire to keep things quiet, the gossip surrounding his termination was considerable. Everyone heard some corrupted version of the story. Allen's first fear—that the accusation be known—was realized. Allen didn't do the terrible thing—rape—he was accused of doing; what he did was stupid enough—having an affair with another employee—but not criminal. In short, his reputation was damaged for the *wrong* reason. And by slinking away like a thief in the night, Allen didn't save his reputation and can't put the past to rest. Now he's got two problems, not just one.

Allen's may be an extreme case, or it may not be. Innocent employees have been railroaded by shortsighted, scandal-fearing bosses, and some employees have participated in their own downfall because they believed exile was the proper punishment for real or imagined indiscretions.

In any event, Allen's decision to do nothing about his assistant's letters was misguided for several reasons. Obviously, had he gotten over his reluctance to discuss the matter with his company and had shown them the letters, he would have been offered either reinstatement or more money to leave quietly.

Allen's belief that if he did nothing about the incident, his reputation would be preserved, is also false. Despite the company's natural desire to keep the situation quiet, leaks about things like this spread like oil spilled from a beached tanker. By the age-old telephone game in which rumors are amplified, distorted, recomposed, and given the widest distribution, Allen's reputation within and, almost certainly, outside the company long ago was trashed. If, on the other hand, Allen had moved to clear himself, even if he didn't retain his job, his departure package would have been greater. His employer acted precipitously in failing to investigate Allen's side of the story—a good beginning for a wrongful termination action.

Another result of Allen's reluctance to deal with his problem is that his personnel record undoubtedly shows he was dismissed *for misconduct*. As we've discussed previously, this information, uncorrected, can pop up at any time to poison job opportunities, promotions, transfers, and awards that Allen might have been scheduled to receive in the future.

Finally, Allen's refusal to resolve the situation using every means at his command may have long-term negative psychological effects on him. Unresolved situations like these don't go away; they hang around forever, causing great unhappiness.

Whether you've responded to your termination by actively negotiating your exit or by passively going with the flow, there's no way to avoid being upset by what happened. If you rise to the challenge, you'll still feel hurt, but you'll also feel empowered at the same time. If you remain passive, you'll feel hurt and, worse, weakened and fearful of the future. So, rise to the challenge. A new job, like a new love after your old love has dumped you, will ease the pain considerably.

If, after everything, you're still troubled by your termination, and this trouble is affecting your work and life, it's time to speak with a professional. Short-term, problem-solving therapy is extremely effective. Your objective is to understand your own thinking and behavior leading up to the termination, to be clear about what you'll need to do in the future.

A final word: Implementing the strategies we've proposed in this book takes courage, especially if you've lived much of your life respecting authority and authority figures. We're not suggesting that you reverse your attitude and begin displaying disrespect. Legitimate authority should be highly regarded, but not blindly, and not as a mask for ignorance or cowardice. Standing up for yourself might result in getting what you want ("The squeaky wheel gets the grease"), or getting yourself bonked ("The nail that sticks out gets the hammer"). The determining factor will be the knowledge you bring to your negotiations. In every instance, thorough preparation—doing your homework—will enhance the power of your case. Moreover, it gives you confidence, the essential element you'll need to bring your courageous actions to success.

# INDEX

# ABOUT THE AUTHORS

**Jodie-Beth Galos** is an attorney and consultant with over twenty years' experience as a senior corporate officer and counsel. She has been associated with a national labor law practice and served as senior vice president of a major financial services corporation, directing its retail human resources and quality departments. Ms. Galos also serves as an arbitrator. She is a graduate of Barnard College, Columbia University, and the Boston University School of Law.

    **Sandy McIntosh** is a writer whose forays into corporate America have been documented in the *Wall Street Journal, Newsday,* and other publications. He is an author of best-selling computer programs, an award-winning screenplay, and four collections of poetry. Mr. McIntosh earned his B.A. from Long Island University, his M.F.A. from Columbia University, and his Ph.D. from the Union Graduate School.

# TWO NOTES TO THE READER
# FROM THE AUTHORS

## ANY QUESTIONS?

We've designed *Firing Back* as a self-help tool. We've explained strategies clearly and provided illustrative examples of how our thinking might be applied to each individual's situation. And, we've cautioned our readers to obtain supporting professional counsel when appropriate.

But you might also have a question we have not answered in the book. If that's the case, we'd like to hear from you.

E-mail us your question at: questions@Firingback.com or fax us directly in New York at: (516) 766-4574

Either way, we'll be happy to answer you personally at no charge.

If we think your question involves more than a swift response to a concise inquiry, we'll suggest how you might obtain more extensive counsel.

## SEMINARS AVAILABLE

Now that you've read *Firing Back*, seminars are available to help you implement the strategies we've outlined in the book. If you have a group that may be interested in a seminar on the issues we discuss in *Firing Back*, you can contact us directly by Fax or e-mail.

We look forward to hearing from you.

Be sure to visit our Web page at http://www.firingback.com for up-to-date news and answers to your questions.